WHEN YOU INTERMARRY

CHARLES J. JOANIDES, PH.D., LMFT

WHEN YOU INTERMARRY:
A Resource for Inter-Christian, Intercultural Couples,
Parents and Families

Foreword by
DEMETRIOS TRAKATELLIS
Archbishop of America

GREEK ORTHODOX ARCHDIOCESE OF AMERICA
New York, New York

ISBN 1-58438-099-3

To My Beautiful Bride

CONTENTS

FOREWORD xiii
ACKNOWLEDGMENTS xvii
INTRODUCTION xix

GENERAL INFORMATION ABOUT INTERMARRIAGES
    Today Intermarriage Is More Acceptable 1
    Some Statistics 2
    Why Intermarriage Is on the Increase 3
    Successful and Unsuccessful Intermarriages 3
HOW INTER-CHRISTIAN COUPLES VIEW RELIGION
    The Value of Religion 6
    Summary 8

WHY INTERMARRIED COUPLES DO NOT ALWAYS
BECOME SINGLE-CHURCH COUPLES
    Familiarity with Religious Tradition 9
    Doctrinal Differences 10
    Ethnic Ties 11
    Weak Religious and Ethnic Attachments 12
    Fear of Betraying Family and/or Background 13
    Growing Up in an Intermarried Home 15
    Minimal Extended Family Pressures 15
    A Personal Decision 16
    Respecting God's Will 16
    Inclusive World View 17
    Social Acceptance 17
    Age 18
    Additional Reasons 18
    Summary 19

WHY INTERMARRIED COUPLES BECOME SINGLE-CHURCH COUPLES
Sources of Contention Eliminated 20
Time, Tolerance, and Education 21
Respectfully Sharing Greek Orthodoxy 22
Weak Religious and Ethnic Connections 23
The Arrival of Children 24
A Love of Orthodoxy 24
Summary 25

HOW INTERMARRIED COUPLES SEE THEIR MARRIAGES
The Up Side 27
The Down Side 29
Summary 31

PARENTING CHALLENGES
Premarital Discussions 32
*Emphasizing Greek Orthodox and Non-Orthodox
Christian Perspectives* 34
Naming the Children 35
Baptizing the Children 36
Reasons Affecting the Parents' Decision to Baptize 37
The "Odd Person Out" 39
When Parents Disagree 40
Living in a Multicultural Society 41
Explaining Intermarriage to the Children 43
The Religious Identity of the Children 44
Help from the Church 45
Intergenerational Differences 46
Boundary Issues 46
Church Attendance by Children 47
Viewing Challenges in Positive Terms 48
Summary 48

EXTENDED FAMILY CHALLENGES
Dating and the Adjustment Period After Marriage 51
Pressures to Wed in the Greek Orthodox Church 55
Pressure Lessens Before Marriage 56

After the Honeymoon and Greek Orthodox
Extended Families 57
After the Honeymoon and the Non-Orthodox Partner 58
Non-Orthodox Extended Family Reactions
to the Orthodox Church 59
Drawing Clear Boundaries 60
Summary 61

ACQUIRING A BETTER UNDERSTANDING OF UNIQUE CHALLENGES
FACED BY INTERMARRIED COUPLES
    Principal Individual Needs 64
    Principal Couple Needs 67
    Balancing Individual and Couple Needs 68
    Some Observations 69
    Martha and Gus 69
    Some Observations 70
    Principal Nuclear Family Needs 70
    Sam and Fran's Failed Attempts at Balancing
    Individual, Couple and Family Needs 74
    Some Additional Observations 75
    Principal Extended Family Needs 75
    Balancing Individual, Couple and
    Extended Family Needs 76
    John and Mary 77
    Some Observations 79
    Balancing Individual, Couple, Children's
    and Extended Family Needs 79
    Bob and Sophia 80
    Some Observations 80
    Faith Community Needs 80
    Jean and George 81
    Some Observations 81
    When Dominant American Cultural Values
    Conflict with Spouses' Subcultural Needs 82
    Sally and Plato 82
    Some Observations 83

MARITAL AND FAMILY LIFE CYCLE CHALLENGES
    Challenges of Inter-Christian, Intercultural Dating 86
    Challenges Dating Couples Might Face 88
    Couple Challenges After Marriage 89
    Meet Tina and Harold 89
    Challenges After Marriage 91
    When the Children Arrive 92
    Meet Bill and Maria 92
    Challenges Related to Starting a Family 95
    When the Children Begin Maturing 97
    Challenges Related to Maturing
    Children's Religious Needs 99
    When Children Reach Adolescence 101
    Challenges Related to Adolescence 103
    When Children Begin Leaving Home 105
    Challenges Related to Young Adulthood 107
    After the Last Child Has Left Home 109
    Challenges After the Last Child Leaves Home 111
    Summary 112

BALANCING STRATEGIES
    Premarital Discussions 113
    Communication After Marriage 114
    A Work in Progress 115
    Patience 115
    A Spirit of Exploration and Experimentation 116
    Mutual Love 117
    Acceptance 117
    A Minimizing/Maximizing Process 118
    Compromise 119
    Humor 119
    Fairness 120
    Freedom to Choose 120
    Healthy Boundaries 121
    Praying Together 122
    Summary 122

INTRODUCTION TO PASTORAL DIRECTIVES
    Pastoral Directives 125

THE VALUE OF PREMARITIAL PREPARATION

Question 1. Have we prayerfully discussed
the pros and cons of entering into an inter-Christian
marriage versus a single-church marriage? 130
Question 2. Have we prayerfully discussed
the pros and cons of becoming an inter-Christian family
versus a single-church family? 132
Question 3. Have I been entirely honest with myself
about entering an inter-Christian marriage? 133
Question 4. Have I been entirely honest with
my spouse about entering an inter-Christian marriage? .. 135
Question 5. How do I meet my personal religious
and spiritual needs in an inter-Christian marriage? 136
Question 6. Is it necessary to be acquainted with
my spouse's religious tradition? 138
Question 7. Will we worship together or apart? 139
Question 8. How do inter-Christian couples that have
equally strong religious commitments decide whether
they will worship apart or together? 139
Question 9. When one spouse has a strong religious
commitment and the other has a weak religious
commitment what are some typical challenges these
couples may encounter? 141
Question 10. Where will we pledge? 143
Question 11. How much of a Greek Orthodox
home will we have? 144
Question 12. In which faith tradition will
the children be baptized? 144
Question 13. How do we help our children
acquire a strong religious identity? 146
Question 14. How do we deal with the questions our
children will have about our inter-Christian marriage? 147
Question 15. Will our ethnic and cultural differences
present us with any challenges? 149
Assessing Your Readiness to Intermarry 150

EPILOGUE 157
SUGGESTED RESOURCES 159
NOTES 161

Each day, in some way, through some relationship, event, conversation, or thought, each one of us is confronted with the challenges and complexities of living in our contemporary world. International and national events, modern American society, religion, culture, and family, personal struggles and ambitions—all of these and many others combine to create issues that not only require our attention, but also summon our entire being—our physical, mental, and spiritual resources—to respond in some significant manner. This is especially true for couples, parents, and families as each new day brings *new* questions needing answers, *new* crises to be overcome, and *new* experiences that can be burdensome, beneficial, and/or life-changing. In addition, clergy and parish leaders who are guiding persons and families in worship, spiritual growth, and service, are confronted by new and multiple issues and are challenged to organize and enhance ministry to meet the needs that arise in our communities, homes, and personal lives.

Evident in our communities and parishes and acknowledged in the pages that follow are a multiplicity of contemporary issues and challenges related to *intermarriage*. The topics that are addressed in this timely work represent genuine needs of couples, parents, and their families as they engage with the vital concerns that arise within the context of marriage between spouses from inter-Christian and intercultural backgrounds. Further, this *Resource Guide* offers information, examples, and counsel to couples and families, as well as to clergy and lay leaders, as they seek direction and answers that will nurture relationships and enhance spiritual, marital, and familial well-being.

This methodical and extensive work, the focus of the Interfaith Research Project of the Greek Archdiocese of America and the vital labor of Father Charles Joanides, reflects our mode of life if we are to live in proper relationship to God and one another in this modern world of rapid movement and constant change. It is in the midst of a very challenging and complex environment that we as Christians must affirm the resolute power of faith and love, as well as the abundant wisdom and spiritual wealth of the Church for guiding our lives and relationships. In his letter to the Ephesians, the Apostle Paul accentuates this manner of living in his discussion of marriage and the Church (Ephesians 5:22-33). In his comparison of the relationship of husband and wife to that of Christ with the Church, he offers a new vista of the depth and significance of these relationships. When he states, *"Husbands love your wives as Christ loved the Church and gave himself up for her"* (5:25), he presents a relationship that is built upon faith, love, selfless sacrifice, and enduring commitment. What is revealed is a bond of communion that has the strength and ability to address any need and overcome any challenge. As applied to intermarriages, this is a mode of daily life and quality relationship that is offered to couples, parents, and their families by a compassionate and saving God. For the Church, the bond between Christ and his people assures us that we will have the resources, the wisdom, the gifts, the ability to meet any challenge or complex issue that has or will be presented in any age.

Thus, in recognition of the sacred strength of the marriage union and in assurance of the transcending capacity for service given to the Church by Christ, this excellent tool for guidance and ministry is offered as a resource for the edification and growth of the people and families of our parishes and as a crucial aid in *equipping* the pastoral ministry of our clergy. The Holy

Archdiocese of America expresses to Father Charles Joanides her sincere appreciation and her warm thanks for this substantive work that will address the needs of its inter-Christian and intercultural marriages. May many lives be blessed through its use, so that families, especially the beloved families of our parishes, become the wonderful and sacred reality that Saint Paul calls the *"church in their house"* (Romans 16:5; I Corinthians 16:19; Colossians 4:15; Philemon 2).

Archbishop Demetrios
Primate of the Greek Orthodox Church in America

ACKNOWLEDGMENTS

Among the numerous individuals who contributed to the completion of this manual, the following individuals deserve special acknowledgment. His Eminence Archbishop Demetrios should be mentioned first since his pastoral guidance permitted and promoted this work. Support and assistance from His Eminence Metropolitan Iakovos, His Eminence Metropolitan Anthony, His Eminence Metropolitan Maximos, His Eminence Metropolitan Methodios, His Eminence Metropolitan Isaiah, His Grace Bishop Alexios, and His Grace Bishop Nicholas must also be mentioned since their guidance facilitated this work's completion in a timely manner. Rosemary Hendrix, Dr. Floyd Hendrix, Marilyn Rouvelas, Sub-deacon Nicholas and Nancy Tentzeras, Beryl Wells Hamilton, Dr. Lewis Patsavos and Dr. Anton Vrame deserve special thanks for their many hours of editing and continued encouragement. In alphabetical order, the following individuals should also be thanked for their many excellent editorial insights: Rev. Fr. Peter Cade, Dr. Chris Granias, Dr. Peter Kalellis, Rev. Fr. Elias Kozar, Phyllis Meshel Onest, Rev. Fr. Polycarpos Rameas and Eric Winger. Gratitude is also extended to Dr. Mick Mayhew for his work as the IRP's research process auditor, and Dr. Philip Mamalakis for his independent analysis of several focus group transcripts. Additionally, and in alphabetical order, Fathers Peter Cade, Paul Costopoulos, William Chiganos, Louis Christopulos, Demetrios Kavadas, Michael Kouremetis, Konstantine Mendrinos, James Paris, Sarantos Serviou, Dennis Strouzas and Elias Velonis should be acknowledged and thanked for agreeing to host focus groups. Fathers Stavros Akrotirianakis, George Alexson,

xvii

Peter Cade, John Chakos, William Chiganos, Louis Christopulos, Paul Costopoulos, Athanasios Demos, Steven Denas, Emmanuel Gratsias, Nicholas Harbatis, Dean Hountalas, Basil Kissal, Michael Kouremetis, Leo Kopacha, John Kutulas, Nicholas Kyritses, Demetrios Kavadas, Kosta Makrinos, Konstantine Mendrinos, Paul Palesty, Stylianos Papanikolaou, Nicholas Papedo, James Paris, Constantine Pavlakos, John Rallis, Kyriakos Saravelas, George Scoulas, Sarantos Serviou, Dennis Strouzas, John Tavlarides, Elias Velonis, Harry Vulopas must also be mentioned for helping to recruit focus group participants. Theo Nicolakis should also be thanked for his many contributions to the Interfaith Marriage Website. My loving wife Nancy and two children Stephan and Sara also deserve my gratitude for their patience as I labored to complete this work. And finally, while it is impossible to personally mention every intermarried spouse who contributed to the thick, rich descriptions and observations contained in this resource, a special mention is offered to the 376 respondents who willingly participated in one of the focus groups, and/or reviewed the information on the Interfaith Marriage Website http://interfaith.goarch.org/ and provided feedback.

In XC,
Rev. Fr. Charles Joanides, Ph.D., LMFT

INTRODUCTION

Therefore a man leaves his father and mother and cleaves to his wife, and they become one flesh - *Gen 2:24.*

Two are better than one, because they have a good reward for their toil. For if they fall, one will lift up his fellow; but woe to him who is alone when he falls and has not another to lift him up. Again, if two lie together, they are warm; but how can one be warm alone? - *Eccl 4:9-11.*

All couples enter their marriages with many hopes and dreams. They may hope to strengthen their love with a lifetime commitment and may dream of a family that provides security and happiness. Wisely, they choose the institution of marriage to fulfill those goals. With the blessings of God, their families, and society, they begin their life together.

The Greek Orthodox Archdiocese of America (GOA), in loving understanding of such hopes and dreams, offers its assistance to help couples cultivate a holy, healthy, marital and family environment. The Church provides this guidebook to facilitate understanding and communication about some of the many challenges couples face.

Often a couple brings different religious and cultural backgrounds to the marriage. In fact, approximately two-thirds (64%) of all marriages conducted across the Greek Orthodox Archdiocese of America are inter-Christian, and in most instances, inter-Christian and intercultural. This guidebook addresses the needs of this growing population of marriages and families referred to in this text as inter-Christian, intermarried or inter-Christian, intercultural couples.[1]

The Interfaith Research Project[2]

Because of the large numbers of inter-Christian marriages conducted in the GOA, an Interfaith Research Project (IRP) was recently conducted to study this growing population of faithful. With the exception of chapters one and ten, the remainder of this book will offer information from 376 intermarried couples that participated in the IRP. These chapters will contain specific information about intermarried couples where one spouse is Greek Orthodox and the other spouse is from another Christian, and in most cases, cultural tradition. These chapters will also concern themselves with couples where at least one spouse attended a Greek Orthodox Church. By becoming familiar with the information that follows, couples will begin to understand that the challenges they face related to their religious and cultural differences are similar to what other couples like themselves have experienced. This information will also assist them in viewing their religious and cultural differences as an opportunity for growth rather than a threat to personal, marital, and family well-being.

Topics Covered in This Book

• General information about intermarriage.
• Descriptions and observations from 376 intermarried spouses who participated in the IRP.
• Useful information that will identify some of the unique challenges that intermarried couples face as spouses, couples, and parents.
• Useful information that intermarried couples and families may encounter in their efforts to worship in the Greek Orthodox Church.
• Useful balancing strategies that have proven to facilitate

marital satisfaction and family well-being in the individual, marital, and family lives of 376 successful intermarried couples.

• Pastoral directives to clarify the Greek Orthodox Church's rules as they apply to intermarried couples.

• Premarital preparation materials written for couples intending to intermarry.

How to Use This Book

• Clergy may recommend this text to conflicted intermarried couples.

• Intermarried couples can review these materials in order to obtain useful information to assist them in their efforts to enhance marital and family stability.

• Intermarried couples, conflicted over their religious and cultural differences, may utilize this book to help them resolve their religious and cultural differences.

• Couples with children can benefit from the information dedicated to the parenting challenges that intermarried couples face.

The most productive way to utilize this book is if both spouses review and discuss these materials together. However, if this is not possible, one spouse may review these materials and can choose to either share the information with his or her partner or unilaterally implement some of the suggestions and balancing strategies. Whichever way the information is utilized, it is expected that the knowledge and implementation of these materials will positively enrich marital and family well-being.

Chapter One

There is no relationship between human beings so close as that of husband and wife, if they are united as they ought to be. – *St. John Chrysostom*

Modern technologies have fostered a global society. People are more interconnected than ever before. Metaphors such as our "spaceship earth" and the "global marketplace" allude to the shrinking, interconnected, interdependent character of contemporary life. As such, national, ethnic, religious, racial, and class boundaries have become more permeable, and people are tending to mix more than ever before. One clear example of all the mixing taking place can be seen when marriage trends in our society are examined more carefully.

Today Intermarriage Is More Acceptable
Up until recently, society held a jaundiced view of intermarriages. Most intermarriages tended to be viewed as an uncommon choice and a betrayal of family and tradition.

Conventional thinking was that intermarried spouses' differing values, food preferences, male and female role perceptions, religious affiliations, child-rearing philosophies, language, and communication styles threatened marital satisfaction. Moreover, it should be noted here that up until recently most church and lay leaders generally held these views across the Greek Orthodox Archdiocese.[1]

1

Social scientists also perceived intermarriages in unflattering terms, and essentially sought to discover how spouses' intercultural differences negatively impacted marital and family life. As a result, scholars alluded to intermarriages' higher divorce rates and tended to describe children from these marriages as living difficult lives.

Over the past decades most scholars studying intermarriage have adopted a much more positive attitude toward these relationships and have begun to emphasize their healthy, functional side. This new generation of scholars has begun to argue that intermarriages do not simply survive, but rather the majority seems to thrive.

Researchers and theorists have also pointed out that the children of intermarriages benefit from being raised in an intercultural family environment. Their lives are generally enriched and their perception of the world is broadened. They have also asserted that successful intermarried couples deal with their cultural, religious and racial differences just as they deal with other differences such as age, gender, and personal preferences and idiosyncrasies.

Some Statistics

Demographically, studies show that inter-ethnic marriages are the most common, followed by inter-Christian/interfaith[2] marriages and interracial marriages with inter-class marriages being comparatively rare. In addition, intermarriage rates vary from region to region in our country.

It is estimated that Protestant groups such as Methodists, Lutherans, Presbyterians and Episcopalians appear to intermarry at a rate of 40-60%. Members of Evangelical Christian denominations such as the Assembly of God, Baptists and the Church of Christ tend to intermarry at about a 40% rate. Statistics also suggest that groups such as Roman Catholics and Jews, who were once believed to be impervious to these trends, are intermarrying at a rate of 30-50%. Recent statistics also indicate that 40% of children born to one Asian parent have a white parent. Hispanic/non-Hispanic marriages in the United States have also doubled since 1970; while marriages between blacks and whites have tripled.

In short, when contemporary generations are compared with previous generations, statistics show that people are crossing over social boundaries with greater frequency. Furthermore, there is nothing to suggest that these trends will reverse themselves in the future. In fact, social scientists studying these trends maintain that the tendency to cross over ethnic, religious, racial, and class boundaries will continue to increase.

Why Intermarriage Is on the Increase

When there are high concentrations of marriageable singles from a given ethnic, religious, or racial group, these regional demographics will tend to reduce the numbers of singles choosing to intermarry. Conversely, when ethnic, religious and racial groups are in a decided minority within a given region of the country, then members of these groups are more likely to intermarry.

In addition, present generations have more opportunities than ever to interrelate and interact with one another. Today, more and more young people are pursuing a higher education. It is also necessary for business people to network across ethnic and national boundaries. More people are moving into the suburbs, and concepts such as respect, tolerance and acceptance for differences are repeatedly applauded. These trends have made it easier for people of marriageable age to meet, date, and marry those outside of their ethnic, religious, racial, and class groups.

Successful and Unsuccessful Intermarriages

As contemporary social scientists seek to find ways of examining intermarriages, one fruitful avenue of research that some experts have utilized has been to compare and contrast unsuccessful intermarriages with successful intermarriages. In general, family scholars have observed that successful intermarried couples generally reach a balanced, complex, rich, and healthy perspective that takes into account their differences and similarities. Scholars have also noted that unsuccessful intermarried couples appear to be stuck in an unbalanced, impoverished, and negatively focused perspective of their marriages. Unsuccessful couples maximize or minimize their differences, ignore their differences completely or view them as liabilities. These observations will become more understandable in the following chapters which feature information from the Interfaith Research Project (IRP).

Chapter Two

Love is patient and kind; love is not jealous or boastful; it is not arrogant or rude. Love does not insist on its own way. – *I Cor. 13:4-5*

Participants in the IRP generally accepted and viewed inter-Christian marriages in a positive light. Conversely, marriages involving non-Christians were generally viewed in a negative light by the IRP couples.

When participants were asked if they might have considered a non-Christian spouse, most believed that the differences were "too great" and the potential problems from these differences might be problematic to couple and family well-being. "My Christian faith is important to me, and so I felt that it was important that I find a Christian to marry. Neither my future wife or I could have continued to grow spiritually in a marriage where both partners belong to a different religion," stated one participant. There appeared to be a general consensus among respondents that they would not consider entering into a marriage with a non-Christian since the religious and cultural differences are greater than they could tolerate and have a greater potential to cause marital instability. They also reasoned that such a decision might disturb their parents and negatively impact their children's perception of religion and culture. "Besides the couple difficulties," said another from the group, "I think extended family difficulties and the challenges of raising children might be intolerable.... I just don't see how you can raise children to be religious in an inter-religious marriage.… And besides, I don't even think that my parents would have accepted such a marriage."

The Value of Religion

Most intermarried spouses and couples who participated in the IRP seemed to place a moderate to high value on religion and spirituality. The following was typical of how respondents felt about religion.[1]

Participants' observations generally suggested that religion has a positive impact on their individual, couple and familial well-being. For example, one respondent stated, "Yes, religion is important. I see how it has helped us and our kids." From another respondent, "Religion kind of completes the family. It's wonderful to wake up every Sunday and go to church. It makes us feel like a family… Call it old-fashioned, but if you look at people and families who are succeeding, they seem to be religious. The people who give up their religion appear to have more problems."

They also remarked that religion assisted them in their efforts to understand and cope with the predictable and unpredictable occurrences that they faced from day to day. "My religion has become part of me," said one participant, "and it gives meaning and purpose to all the difficult stuff that I have to deal with every day." In another instance, another respondent stated, "Recently, I lost my father unexpectedly, and my faith really helped me with that loss. It brings me comfort to know that he is with God now."

Respondents' comments also inferred that religion provided each member of the family with a moral foundation, as well as providing the family with a collective moral grounding. "It helps teach right and wrong, and it gives the family a moral foundation in an otherwise crazy world," stated one person. In another instance, a member said, "What's wrong with family life today is that families have lost sight of the moral underpinnings that religion offers people."

They also observed that organized religion provides a ready-made structure that family members can utilize to worship God as individuals, couples and as a family. "Religion provides my prayer life with needed structure," said one. Another observed, "It's a kind of foundation or structure that helps our marriage and the family worship God."

Participants also alluded to the personal and private side of their religious experience with frequency, and suggested that in many instances, it was this side of their religious experiences that promoted church attendance. For example, consider the following excerpt from one respondent's observations. "When I'm in church, I sometimes go to a 'place' where only God and I are. This place doesn't involve others around me per se. It's just a place where I know He is, and I can feel His presence. It's like a private place where I can sort of sit in His lap and be His kid for a while."

Religion was also likened to "a glue" that keeps intermarried couples connected to each other and to their extended families. "When we come to the Greek Church, we come together, and we meet my wife's family. This is good, because it's another way that helps us keep that family togetherness that so many families lack these days in our fast-paced world."

Religion was also repeatedly observed to keep inter-Christian couples connected with other people of similar religious beliefs. One respondent offered, "You go downstairs on Sunday after liturgy and there are bagels and coffee and friendly faces and you can talk with people of like mind and feel as if you are speaking the same language." In another instance, another remarked, "there's a common ground experience that I feel when I come to church. Out there in the world, it's all me, me, me, and take, take, take. However, when I come here, I feel like the rules are different because everyone has just listened to a sermon and prayed. It's a good feeling."

Religious affiliation also tended to meet some or all participants' social needs. "We know everyone here, and my wife's family is here, so it's a good place to meet the people you know, and also meet new people." This seemed especially true of participants who lived in large urban areas such as New York and Chicago. In these instances, membership and participation in a church were paralleled to "belonging to a small town in a big city, where people could feel a greater social connection to one another, sort of like being a part of a small town I would imagine."

Religion was also repeatedly viewed by most participants as playing a central role in forming their sense of self. Addressing this issue, one respondent said, "my religion has played a major role in forming me, and it's at the core of who I am." Another said, "I come here because it's a part of me, and I'm a part of it."

Summary

Most participants from the IRP viewed inter-Christian marriages in positive terms, but were not as inclined to view inter-religious marriages in a similar manner. They perceived the differences in an inter-religious marriage to be too difficult to negotiate. Most participants also placed a high value on religion and spirituality. They believed that religion and spirituality enriched their lives in numerous ways. As a result, these participants sought to cultivate individual, couple and family religious and spiritual well-being.

Chapter Three

But the fruit of the Spirit is love, joy, peace, patience, kind-
ness, goodness, faithfulness, gentleness, self-control. – *Gal.* 5:22

And above all these put on love, which binds everything
together in perfect harmony. – *Col.* 3:14

While many of the couples that participated in the IRP attended the Orthodox Church and were raising their children in
the Orthodox Church, most had also chosen to remain intermarried. There are many good reasons why these couples had
made this choice. The reasons listed below were most frequently
mentioned.

Familiarity with Religious Tradition
Many participants' observations and descriptions indicated
that they placed a high value on retaining membership in their
own religious and cultural tradition because they were most
familiar with their religious background. They repeatedly stated
that they could not imagine themselves belonging to another
faith tradition other than their own. Statements such as the following from both Greek Orthodox and non-Orthodox participants were shared:
"I feel very close to Orthodoxy... but I could never consider
converting."

9

"I just feel as if my Protestant faith is still something I want to hang onto. And that's that. I guess down deep, I'm still Protestant."

"I'm Catholic, and I couldn't imagine being anything but Catholic."

When pressed to elaborate further, many described a familiarity, affection, and comfort with their religious tradition that was integrally important to their efforts to worship God. One participant stated, "I enjoy singing certain Protestant hymns. They allow me to get into the right spirit." In another focus group, a Catholic participant stated, "I like going to the Catholic Church because I know what's going on. I get to participate more with the priest, instead of just standing there and listening to someone else chant."

Participants also stated that their lack of familiarity with their partner's religious tradition tended to stifle their efforts to worship at the same intimate level. A Greek Orthodox participant said, "I tried going to my spouse's church, but it just didn't do anything for me. I guess I need to hear the chanting, see the icons, and smell the incense." The following remarks by a Catholic participant were also typical of how many non-Orthodox felt about their Greek Orthodox partner's faith tradition. "When I go to the Catholic Church, I know the mass by heart and what's going to happen next. It's not like that when I attend the Greek Church." To that end, numerous participants in this study tended to view conversion as a risky option that might serve to compromise or impair their religious and spiritual development, as well as their relationship with God. "I guess I'm happy where I am," said one. "If I decided to change, I just don't know how that might affect my relationship with God."

Doctrinal Differences

Participants' discomfort with some of the doctrinal differences that existed between their religious traditions were also occasionally alluded to as factors that inhibited them from considering conversion. "I just don't understand icons. I've been told that they're holy objects that stimulate prayer, but my religious background taught me to believe that this sort of thing is a form of idolatry. So, I just can't seem to get past what I've learned about idol worship when I'm around icon." Conversely, in other instances some of the Greek Orthodox participants stated that their non-Orthodox partner's faith tradition sometimes had ambiguous rules and guidelines. "At least I kind of know where my church stands on certain moral and Church issues, even though I may not always agree. Some churches' positions on issues like abortion, women priests, for example, are too rigid or too fuzzy, and that bothers me."

Ethnic Ties

Those who participated in the IRP often conceptualized Greek Orthodoxy in ethno-religious[1] terms. The following comments exemplify this point. "I just don't think you can take the Greek out of my experiences when I come to church. There's a cultural and religious blending that I experience and I don't feel like they can be separated." Several non-Greek Orthodox spouses with strong ethnic attachments stated that their moderate to strong ethnic ties prevented them from considering conversion. For example, one respondent said, "Thinking about converting is a very emotional subject for me. Whenever I consider this idea, I think about my ethnic background and know that I could not convert because you almost have to become a little Greek to belong to this Church, and that would mean I would have to become a little less Brazilian."

Such participants associated conversion with a loss of a fundamental and important part of themselves. The following comments are indicative of what numerous respondents stated: "If I were to leave the Church, I would feel like I was leaving something important about who I am and what makes me tick.... A large part of why I go to the Greek Church is because I am Greek, and my Greek heritage means something to me." Elsewhere another participant stated, "thinking about conversion is like thinking about uprooting something that is central to who you are, in my case, my Panamanian Catholic background. In a sense, for a person like myself who has strong ethnic and religious roots, becoming Greek Orthodox feels as if I am opting to become a slightly different person, with a different mentality. Therefore, I stay where I am, and how I grew up because that makes me feel comfortable... My religious and ethnic background is at the root of who I am. You just can't take these roots out and say, 'we are going to put you in another place.' If I were to change or convert I personally feel that I would be a different person."

Weak Religious and Ethnic Attachments
Observations from spouses with equally low levels of religious and cultural commitment tended to be different from those with a moderate to high level of commitment. When spouses' religious traditions and cultures did not play prominent roles in their lives, this factor often inhibited them from considering conversion. Specifically, results from the IRP suggest that spouses with low levels of religious and/or ethnic commitment have very little incentive to become a single-church couple because religion plays a peripheral role in their lives. These respondents further stated that making any changes in their religious status did not seem to them to be "cost effective," since conversion requires "time" and "effort" and, "a commitment to a way of living and thinking that may not always fit with our current world view."

On the other hand, nominally religious participants often admitted that since religion did not play a role in their lives, their mate's religious affiliation was not a chief consideration during the dating process, nor was their mate's religious affiliation perceived as playing a primary role in their marriage's well-being. Other factors such as their spouse's personality, family values, world view, and their mutual love for one another were mentioned as being more important reasons to explain why they were attracted to their mate, why they chose to marry their spouse, and why they remained married. One spouse's remarks are reflective of this. "Even though she's Catholic, when we were dating I looked at the person, her values, her family... and not the religion. Since I'm not real religious, that's what made me feel strongly about marrying her. So I suppose conversion was and will continue to be a non-issue for me personally."

In addition, these respondents maintained that because of their nominal religious and/or cultural attachments, they had not considered conversion because they could not perceive how conversion might improve the quality of their lives. Their observations suggested that their religious and cultural differences were only occasional irritants in their lives that did not justify the effort it might take to convert. "Once in a while, religion comes up as a problem because she's more religious than I am. However, she knows how I feel, and I know how she feels. We find ways of patching up these differences just as we find ways of mending the problems we face that are related to culture, finances, politics, you name it." A different participant offered a similar remark. "I suppose we became an interfaith couple because I wasn't very religious and continue to be indifferent to religious matters." Generally, they inferred that their nominal interest in religion played a role in their decision to become involved in an inter-Christian intercultural marriage, as well as their decision to remain intermarried.

Fear of Betraying Family and/or Background

Converting to another faith tradition was conceptualized by many participants as a type of "renunciation" and "betrayal" of their current belief system. The following observation clearly indicates this point. "About eight years ago I came to church with my husband and there was this man in front of the church converting from Catholicism to Orthodoxy, and the words he repeated during this service just made me grab the pew and squeeze so hard. He said, 'I cast away all errors and false doctrines I have held,' and later I talked to the Father about that, and he said, 'I don't remember that,' but I do. These words echoed in my head, 'I cast out.' How can I cast away or in effect renounce what I was born with, what my family has been for generations? How can I renounce that? I can't. I can't."

In other instances, several considered conversion as an act of "betrayal" and disloyalty to their culture, family, parents, or grandparents. The following are typical responses, which were shared within various groups:

"I really feel strongly about being Greek Orthodox, and to a large extent that's probably because my family is Greek. Conversion would make me feel like I have been disloyal to my family and who they are."

"My family is Irish-Catholic and I feel that I should be Irish-Catholic. Converting would somehow seem as if I was betraying my family."

"My family has been a good Southern family who have been Church of Christ people for as long as anyone can remember. Converting would feel as if I was doing something wrong: almost like renouncing what you are, if you know what I mean."

A concern not to upset or insult extended families was repeatedly mentioned as a factor that discouraged conversion. These participants frequently stated that if they opted to convert, they feared that this decision might somehow hurt their parents and perhaps their grandparents. "My mother is still alive. It's not that I participate as a Protestant anymore, because I attend the Greek Church with my family. However, maybe subconsciously I feel as if converting would hurt her," another participant offered. Respect for family members' feelings were thus often mentioned as either being equally important, or in some cases, more important than the notion of being a one-faith family. "My husband knows how I feel about converting, and he's grown to respect my thoughts and feelings... even though he's the religious one, he knows that my family's feelings are important, and I could never let them down by converting to his church, even though it makes perfect sense in some ways."

Growing Up in an Intermarried Home
   There were some participants who had been raised in an inter-Christian home environment that was both stable and happy. To that end, these individuals concluded that their positive family-of-origin experiences had made it easier for them to choose to enter and remain in an inter-Christian intercultural marriage. One such respondent said, "I grew up in an inter-Christian household. My father was Greek Orthodox and my mother was Catholic. My parents got along really well, and I have nothing but good, happy memories of our home environment. So when I considered getting married, I wasn't fazed by the fact that we weren't going to have the same religion."

Minimal Extended Family Pressures
   When spouses perceived that members from their family of origin did not strongly resist their decision to intermarry, participants indicated it was easier for them to choose to enter and remain intermarried. "If I had gotten the kind of flack from my family that some of the people tonight have described I might have thought twice about marrying someone from another religion. However, my parents were not very concerned about this, so long as she was Christian. As long as she was Christian, it didn't matter. So it was kind of easy for us to ignore the religious issue and just get married." In this case, this respondent seemed to suggest that the minimal family-of-origin pressures he had received regarding intermarriage enabled him to remain indifferent to the notion of conversion.

A Personal Decision
   We live in a society that espouses religious freedom. How one believes and what one believes is ultimately a personal choice.

Participants generally ascribed to this notion. They repeatedly stated that one's religious preference is more of a personal decision and less of a couple's decision. They also frequently alluded to the serious nature of this decision, and observed that conversion should not be considered an option simply to satisfy the Church, their extended families, or their spouse. Conversion must be heartfelt and God-inspired, otherwise future resentments and regrets might develop which could serve to negatively impact the well-being of the marriage. For example, while speaking about many of these issues, a respondent stated, "My husband is Catholic, but he comes to church with us as a family. Moreover, I respect him, and I thank God that we can pray together, and we come to church together as a family. In addition, I respect what is right for him.... I want the best for my husband. And I pray to God that he will do what is right for himself, and that God will direct all of us."

Respecting God's Will

It was not uncommon for participants to assert that they believed it was God's will that they respect each other's religious and cultural differences, and that a failure to do so was interpreted as disrespectful, unholy behavior. The following brief comments from one focus group partcipant is an example of this sentiment. "And I have this feeling, sometimes very strongly, that I would love for him to convert. However, the Lord brought him into this world a Catholic. So, who am I to push my husband to convert to my church, as beautiful and wonderful as I think it is? Therefore, I don't push him to convert, but sometimes I think, well, maybe I should, and we'd be better off. But then again, I just don't feel that's my place."

Inclusive World View

Intermarried couples' broad, inclusive perceptions of their world also appeared to affect how they viewed conversion and single-church marriage. Participants frequently stated that they belonged to a global society that was not nearly as compartmentalized as it once was. Because of this inclusive perception of the world, intermarried couples often place less value on conversion and the notion of a single-church marriage and family. While reflecting on the issue of conversion, one respondent stated, "in my mind, most of the differences between denominations are political and historical more than anything else. Even though my husband is Catholic and I am Greek Orthodox, I believe that we are both part of the same Christian Faith. So, I don't really see the need [to convert], except maybe for the sacraments. However, my husband is Catholic, and receives [communion] in the Catholic Church.... The world is getting smaller, and we have to stop compartmentalizing each other. I believe it's the Christian thing to do." In a different group, another respondent expressed similar sentiments. She stated, "so I think when someone is in the Christian way, under the guidance of Jesus Christ, I don't think there is much difference really, except in the ways that a ceremony goes, or some rules. But the main thing is that we believe in Jesus Christ. As long as my husband believed in Christ, I felt comfortable marrying him."

Social Acceptance

Since intermarriage is socially acceptable in our dominant American culture, and is perceived as workable, many intermarried couples ignore the value of conversion. From one respondent, "we live in different times. The world has shrunk, and people are marrying outside of their groups with more frequency. So that's why I married my wife, and we weren't too concerned about our different religious and ethnic backgrounds."

Age

Research has shown that as people mature, their view of life tends to be less flexible and they tend to be less inclined to make big changes in their lives. Some research on intermarriage has also indicated that the longer couples remain in an inter-Christian and intercultural marriage, the less probable it is that such couples will become single-church couples. Results from this study support and suggest that spouses' age and length of time married tend to discourage thoughts of conversion. One respondent's remarks reflect this. "We've been able to share our two religions to our own satisfaction and our family's satisfaction and our spiritual satisfaction, so now we're content to go along that road after nearly fifteen years."

Additional Reasons

The following reasons for not converting were also mentioned with less frequency:

Some non-Orthodox stated that they had not considered conversion because they were not convinced that Orthodoxy was any better than their own faith tradition. While, others suggested that they had not converted to Greek Orthodoxy because the Greek Orthodox Church they attended had failed to convince them it was interested in having them become part of the Orthodox Church. In these instances, it appeared that some participants might have considered conversion if the subject was broached in a respectful manner.

More information about Greek Orthodoxy also seemed key to non-Orthodox participants with regards to conversion. While many stated that they would likely not convert if given more information, a small but significant number stated that they might consider conversion more seriously if they knew more about Greek Orthodoxy. One respondent stated, "The Greek Orthodox Church tends to be different than most other churches. So I think that's why it's important that churches make it a common habit to offer some regular classes for interested non-Orthodox." Language and cultural differences were also mentioned as factors that prevented some non-Orthodox from considering conversion. Some said that the emphasis on both language and culture would make them feel uncomfortable, and not a part of the Greek Orthodox Church.

While many non-Orthodox participants had chosen not to convert for one or more reasons, several stated that they: came to church regularly; were committed to their churches; and felt like members.

Summary
   In some instances, couples in this study appeared to practice two different faith traditions, while in other instances, spouses belonged to two different faith traditions but were essentially practicing one faith tradition, generally, Greek Orthodoxy.
   And while many of these participants' remarks tended to lament the fact that they could not worship and/or belong to the same cultural and faith tradition, they reported being willing to accept their religious and cultural differences because of their mutual love for one another. The challenges they confronted from being involved in an inter-Christian and intercultural marriage/family were easier to accept than the thought of either not being married or disavowing their religious and cultural backgrounds through conversion. As a result, these couples generally struggled to find ways of bridging their religious and cultural differences, and tended to accept and respect their partner's need to retain membership in his or her cultural and faith tradition. Finding mutually creative and positive ways to retain membership with their cultural and religious tradition was of paramount importance to their marital stability. Since both religion and culture were perceived as intrinsically important to these participants' sense of self, some indicated that they did not fully expect their spouse to change. They further suggested that the inherent qualities that served to make their spouse the unique person that they fell in love with might somehow be altered or disrespected through the conversion process. Several couples did, however, state that they might consider conversion if they perceived that this change might be beneficial to their family's total well-being.

Chapter Four

WHY INTERMARRIED COUPLES BECOME SINGLE-CHURCH COUPLES

The joint prayer of husband and wife is a great force. – *Starets Macarius*

A pure and honorable marriage, in the fear of God, is indeed a vessel of the Holy Spirit. – *St. Nicholas of Zhicha*

One of the defining characteristics of Orthodoxy is that it is a faith that values, above almost everything else, a person's freedom to choose. Since freedom is inherently central to our conception of God, and since God created us with free will and He does not violate our free will, the Orthodox Church believes that conversion must come from the heart and cannot be forced. To that end, the following information is offered respectfully and in an effort to cultivate healthy conversions and discourage those conversions that occur for the wrong reasons.[1]

Although most participants involved in the IRP appeared to be very comfortable with their decision to intermarry, there were a small number of participants in this study (11%) who were considering conversion. Intermarried couples that were considering this option were generally motivated to do so for one or more of the following reasons.

Sources of Contention Eliminated

When compared with their parents, research indicates that Baby Boomers and Generation Xers are less likely to become single-church couples. Despite this finding, results from the IRP suggest that a small but sizeable number of contemporary inter-Christian spouses believe that conversion can positively impact their marriage. In these cases, these spouses were leaning toward conversion and asserted that conversion would likely strengthen their marriage by removing possible sources of contention that could compromise spousal and extended family stability. The following comments made by one participant illustrate these points, "Since I was married before, I wanted this marriage to work, and if making it work meant that I convert so that the family is happy, well – so be it. Therefore, I'm going to convert. But I want you to know that I'm not being pressured into making this decision, but I'm doing it out of a desire to do the Christian thing." In another group, another respondent stated, "Staying happy is hard enough for couples these days. So, I'm beginning to lean toward conversion. I figure it might eliminate some of the possible problems that could result, and maybe even bring us closer as a family."

Time, Tolerance, and Education
    Time, tolerance, additional information, and education classes appeared to be invaluable in helping intermarried couples decide if they should become single-church couples. "What I needed was some space to make the decision," stated one respondent who was embracing Orthodoxy in the near future. "In my heart of hearts, I always knew that I would convert, but if someone had pressured me, that wouldn't have been good." These spouses stated that if they felt forced, manipulated, or made to feel guilty, they imagined that these types of tactics would have proven counterproductive to the conversion process. The following exchange between two spouses further illustrates this point.
    "If I felt pushed, I might have eventually relented, but I also imagine that I would have ultimately begun feeling resentful and resistant. By allowing me the space to make my own decision, I feel like it was a more personal and more meaningful

decision. And that's the way it should be – conversion should be a personal decision."

"I would agree. I knew that if I had somehow forced the issue, and determined not to marry him unless he converted, he might have given in and become Orthodox. But I also kind of knew that this would be a bad way to start out our marriage. And besides, I wouldn't want anyone to have used these tactics on me."

Respectfully Sharing Greek Orthodoxy

If a non-Orthodox spouse is approached respectfully and sincerely with the idea of conversion, and if the individual approached discerns that he/she is not being proselytized, this evangelical approach can facilitate conversion. For example, one participant stated, "I never forced him. It was his decision. I respected him and knew if I had tried to push, that it would have been harmful to our marriage. It was his decision, not mine. He was the one that had to feel like that's what God wanted for our family."

However, the flip side of being respectful is being so respectful that non-Orthodox are not extended an invitation to convert. "For the longest time," stated one respondent, "I thought that I wasn't welcome to join. And all I could come up with for a reason is that I wasn't Greek. Then one day as I was talking with Fr. Nick, he politely said to me, 'Sam, I noticed that you've been coming regularly. Why haven't you thought about conversion?' and that started me to thinking that maybe I was welcome." Speaking from a similar perspective, a Greek Orthodox participant stated, "We don't make the same kind of effort to evangelize the non-Orthodox that visit our churches as other churches do. I guess we're too respectful, or maybe it's not that simple... Maybe we're just not used to doing this, and most of us don't know how to reach out and respectfully extend non-Orthodox an invitation to consider becoming part of the Church. But we should. I think that's God's work, and I think that more people might respond to conversion if they felt that they are welcomed and they are approached in a proper way." When non-Orthodox genuinely perceive that there is a place for them in the Orthodox Church, and that their conversion is welcomed by the congregation and priest, conversion is sometimes considered an option.

Weak Religious and Ethnic Connections
A weak connection to one's religious tradition, together with a renewed sense of the importance of religion, made it easier for some participants to consider conversion. "I wasn't very religious when we first got married. As I got older, and my priorities changed, religion seemed to take on more importance for me. Since my wife and kids are Greek Orthodox, it seemed like a natural thing for me to consider the Orthodox Church more seriously. Today I am in the process of going through the Inquirer's Class to enter the Orthodox Church."

Similarly, a weak connection to one's religious tradition, along with the perception that conversion might strengthen one's marriage and enhance one's relationship with one's in-laws also offered enough incentive to consider conversion. For instance, one respondent said, "The main reason why we got married in the Orthodox Church is because this decision was going to help our family. His parents didn't accept me easily because I was previously married, and so I said to myself, this is going to be my mother-in-law, and I want to make this work. So we got married Orthodox, and now I'm considering conversion for some of the same reasons. Besides that, I really didn't have any strong connections to my religion."

In both instances, because some intermarried spouses might lack intimate connection with their religious and/or cultural tradition, converting was easier since the perceived losses appeared minimal or in some cases insignificant as compared to the perceived personal, marital, and family benefits that conversion affords.

It is also important to note that evidence from the IRP suggests that some adult children who were born into and raised in a Greek Orthodox family that was nominally religious but had strong ethnic ties ended up converting to their spouses' faith tradition. In these cases, these participants stated that they would attend their partner's church and would periodically visit the Greek Orthodox Church in an effort to affiliate with their family and the Greek community.

The Arrival of Children

When intermarried couples decide to have children, or when their children begin to mature and are able to ask questions about religion, some couples reconsider their decision to remain in an inter-Christian marriage. For example, one father stated, "I think that it's very important that the kids see both parents go to church... I would sit at home on Sundays. As the kids grew I began to hear them saying, 'why do I have to go, Dad isn't going.' So then, I began to rethink what I was doing, and started going to church regularly. And after a while I also began thinking about maybe even converting." In another instance, a mother stated, "One day after a particularly difficult Sunday morning – the details of which I won't mention – I thought about how blessed we are to have been given two children, and I began thinking about God's will and what He wanted me to do about our religious situation, and it slowly started becoming clear to me that our children needed one church home. So for our children's sake, I've decided to convert." In these instances, some inter-Christian spouses observe that conversion might serve to benefit their families' and children's religious development. Many of these couples' observations suggest that a single-church family is God's will.

A Love of Orthodoxy

Conversion that was coerced or entered into to simply satisfy church rules, the extended family, and/or one's spouse, was repeatedly described in uncomplimentary terms. As such, remarks like the following one were made repeatedly. "I feel very strongly about this. If you don't feel that you should convert – you shouldn't. Moreover, if you feel like you're being pressured, and you convert, what good is that? It might just lead to trouble in the future. What I mean is that the person who converts may end up being resentful." Conversely, having a sincere, heartfelt commitment to the Orthodox faith was perceived as another legitimate, justifiable, and healthy reason to convert. "I didn't convert," stated one respondent, "because Nick wanted it. I converted because I love the Orthodox faith." In another focus group, the following observation was shared. "Before meeting Nicole, I was searching for a church that fit with who I am. So when I met my wife, I not only found a partner, but I also found a church that fit with who I am and how I like to relate to God. I believe that if I hadn't met Nicole, I might eventually still have become Orthodox."

Summary

As couples and families mature, they encounter different needs and challenges. In some instances, personal needs begin to take a back seat to couple and family needs – especially with respects to children's religious and spiritual developmental needs. One respondent stated, "I was convinced to convert because it was more important to me that my kids develop a clear religious identity, than it was for me to continue to be Catholic." Sometimes, the death of a parent or grandparent permits spouses the latitude to consider conversion. "When my mother died, I felt freer to consider my wife's faith. Until then, I didn't want to upset my mother," said another respondent. At other times, spouses' attitudes toward their mates' faith tradition, or a renewed interest in religion, compels couples and spouses to consider conversion. "I just didn't think about conversion one day, it's been a long process," stated one respondent. "Both my increased understanding of Orthodoxy and the value of religion made a big difference in my decision to begin considering conversion." Whatever the reason, results from the IRP suggest that some spouses and couples determine that they and their families will benefit from a decision to become a single-church family.

Chapter Five

Have no anxiety about anything, but in everything by prayer and supplication with thanksgiving let your requests be known to God. And the peace of God, which passes all understanding, will keep your hearts and your minds in Christ Jesus. – *Phil. 4:6-7*

Lord our God, crown them with glory and honor. – *From the Sacrament of Marriage*

The Up Side

Despite the additional difficulties and challenges that inter-Christian married couples face the majority of those who participated in the IRP did not appear to have any major regrets with their decision to intermarry and remain itermarried. The following remarks were typical of how most couples in this study felt about their intermarriages: "I have no regrets, and I wouldn't do it any other way. She has been the best thing that ever happened to me, and our love for one another has helped us make things work."

Most couples did not view their religious and cultural differences as being more significant than other differences they faced, but they were aware that their religious and cultural differences could potentially create marital conflict. Therefore, they worked hard to make certain that these potential sources of

27

conflict would not create additional strife in their marriages. "It's true," said one respondent, "there are some extra challenges, but they haven't been anything we couldn't handle. It just takes a willingness to work things out." Even though they had managed to accept and learn to live with their differences, they still viewed them as potential sources of difficulty that needed periodic attention throughout the marital life cycle. Comments such as "this is a work in progress," and "there are plenty of ways to create problems in an inter-Christian, intercultural marriage" and, "you've got to make the best of things," served to reinforce the need for continued vigilance.

Their competency at finding ways of bridging their differences appeared to be immensely important to their well-being. One spouse, married to someone who was nominally religious, lamented the fact that she attended church services alone on most Sundays. Almost in the same breath, she also remarked that she viewed this time as personal time which afforded her an opportunity "to be with God." Rather than making her spouses' low interest in religion an issue, she found ways of making the best of this challenge and turned a potentially problematic issue into an opportunity for personal growth.

Generally speaking, these participants did not view their religious and cultural differences as serious threats to their marriages' stability. "I've seen other couples that have worse problems than we do as an inter-Christian couple. And really, we don't have it too bad because we know several Orthodox couples that have it worse. It's got a lot to do with the love and commitment you share with each other as far as I'm concerned, and less to do with our religious and cultural differences." They often maintained that these differences were generally of no greater significance than other differences that they faced as couples. Most of these couples (especially the Baby Boomers) had long addressed their differences and found ways of either circumventing them or eliminating them.

Spouses also repeatedly maintained that their religious and cultural diversity functioned to enrich their lives as individuals and as a couple. Comments such as "it's an enriching arrangement" and "I feel richer and not poorer" were generally used to describe their inter-Christian intercultural marriages. Numerous participants observed that their partner's religious tradition provided them with another dimension of Christianity that served to broaden their understanding of their own personal religious tradition. Upon reflecting on his own marriage one respondent said, "We both draw upon very rich traditions, and within each of our traditions there are many, many good things and moments to build upon. This has certainly broadened our understanding of our own and each other's religious tradition." Many participants also described how their partner's cultural/ethnic heritage added richness and variety to their lives. "Two Easter baskets are better than one," and "The different foods, languages, traditions, religious perspectives… they are more enriching than belonging to one faith and one culture… the diversity is the beauty of intermarriage."

Respondents' love for one another, their desire to see their marriages succeed, their interest in maintaining family stability, their respect for diversity, their mutual belief in Christ, and their tolerant and patient attitudes for their respective religious and cultural differences appeared to be indispensable to their efforts to advance marital and family satisfaction and stability.

The Down Side

Although most inter-Christian couples involved in the IRP viewed their intermarriages in basically positive terms, some respondents did indicate that their religious and cultural differences tended to create a wedge between them. Some couples viewed these differences as creating a low to moderate sense of distance between them and their spouses and children. "It's been a challenge and I sometimes feel an emptiness at times when I'm at church alone. And this emptiness, I think, is from feeling a bit distant from my wife and children in this part of our lives." Couples with equally strong commitments to their chosen faith tradition were especially challenged by their religious differences, and maintained that these differences could be detrimental to their marriage. Moreover, this distance created a sense of separation between these couples that was sometimes perceived as unbridgeable. "It's been a challenge, I won't deny it. We're both very faithful, and we both want to practice our faiths rigorously and with regular involvement. So, when I started going to the Greek Church, I got rather resentful and frustrated because it just wasn't the same and I felt deprived of something very important. Moreover, this really affected us for a while and I wondered what the consequences of this would be until I found a way to meet my own spiritual needs. Still, I sometimes wish that things were different, and we weren't from different religious backgrounds."

Speaking about some of the difficulties that their cultural differences created, the following exchange between one couple illustrates how culture can also function to create distance and conflict.

Hank: "It's sometimes been hard for me. I come from a background that isn't very ethnic. So, when I married Maria, it was hard at first because her Greek background is very important to her. I don't necessarily like a lot of the Greek foods she likes, and I was not accustomed to people asking me my personal business or being so emotionally expressive. I mean, we just never raised our voices at each other, or asked the kinds of personal questions that I've been asked when I've visited her family. It's not as bad today. I've gotten used to the way Greek families interact with each other. But for a while, I wondered if Maria's background would affect us, since I wasn't that interested in becoming Greek. But like I've said, we've worked this out, and we have a better understanding about it."

Maria: "That's true. We've come a long way and I've gained some understanding about our cultural preferences. Nevertheless, sometimes I wish that Hank was Greek because I feel as if it's a part of my life that I can't really share with him. In addition, I also wonder about our children because I'd like them to speak Greek and appreciate the Greek culture. I think it will make them better people."

Hank: "It is better than it was," and I am trying. But we have determined to meet each other halfway on this issue. She won't make me Greek, and I won't be irritated at her when she needs to spend some time with other Greeks. As far as the children go, well, my philosophy is that the children will eventually choose. She can introduce them to the culture, and I won't object. But they will eventually choose how Greek they want to be, no matter what we do."

Summary

Most participants indicated that they did not regret being intermarried. They stated that the challenges they faced related to their religious and cultural differences were of no greater significance than other challenges they encountered over such matters such as money, sex and parenting. They clearly believed that their religious and cultural differences functioned to enrich their lives.

Some participants did express some lingering misgivings with their marriages. These respondents' observations suggested that they viewed their religious and cultural differences as potential threats to individual, marital and family stability and satisfaction. Disagreements over food and drink, religion and in-laws were frequently used to describe their dissatisfaction with their marriages.

Time, tolerance and acceptance seemed to reduce tension and increase marital satisfaction for most couples. Some of these participants also alluded to how God's loving, forgiving grace had proven to be invaluable to their efforts to find stability. Their mutual love and their desire to succeed appeared to assist them often in bridging their differences.

Chapter Six

PARENTING CHALLENGES

Let everything take second place to our care for our children, our bringing them up in the discipline of the Lord. If from the beginning we teach them to love true wisdom, they will have greater wealth and glory than riches can provide. – *St. John Chrysostom*

That they may rejoice in the beholding of sons and daughters, let us pray to the Lord. – *From the Sacrament of Marriage*

Because when harmony prevails, the children are raised well, the household is kept in order, and neighbors, friends and relatives praise the result. – *St. John Chrysostom*

When children arrive, marital dynamics change and new challenges must be negotiated. Above and beyond the normal challenges confronting single-church families, inter-church families with children must deal with a host of additional problems. The following information will describe some of the typical and unique challenges that inter-Christian couples face in their efforts to nurture their children in the Greek Orthodox Church.

Premarital Discussions
Numerous participants stated that they had spent some time before their wedding discussing their future children's religious and cultural needs. Questions such as the following played a prominent role in these discussions: In which church will we

baptize our children? Will we nurture our children in both spouses' churches? To what degree will our respective cultural traditions be shared with our children? Which cultural traditions do we want to share with our children?

Participants who had engaged in these discussions initially found that both they and their children had generally profited from taking these questions into consideration. One non-Orthodox participant's remarks exemplify the benefits of premarital discussions: which concern their future children's well-being. "It was a good thing that we engaged in some discussion about our children's religious training. We are both pretty committed to our churches, and it would have created a lot of problems if we hadn't done some thinking about this before marriage. And it was hard stuff to discuss, but we settled it before the wedding and I think it made us a stronger couple after marriage."

Many participants who failed to engage in any premarital discussion regarding their future children's religious and/or cultural development believed that they might have profited from them. In retrospect, most believed that some premarital discussion might have reduced misunderstandings after marriage that was related to the individual spouse's unspoken assumptions regarding his or her children's religious and cultural development. As one respondent stated, "We never talked about which church the children would be raised in until I got pregnant. I guess I just assumed that we were going to raise our children in the Greek Orthodox Church, especially since we got married in the Greek Church. Moreover, when he began to resist this I got really upset. It wasn't that he was totally against the idea, but he wanted to wait and allow us some time to make a decision. Nevertheless, I wanted to make the decision before the baby arrived. In addition, though we eventually baptized her in the Greek Church, we really had some difficulties about this issue that made things kind of tense during the pregnancy and even after the birth. I would advise mixed couples to iron this issue out before marriage especially if they both have strong religious connections."

Emphasizing Greek Orthodox and Non-Orthodox Christian Perspectives
When discussing inter-faith and inter-cultural challenges, an ongoing general struggle that couples often face is how they can remain respectful to their own religious and cultural preferences while also being respectful of their partner's religious and cultural preferences. As such, it should come as no surprise that when intermarried couples decide to have children, striking a balance between their personal religious and cultural preferences, their partner's religious and cultural preferences, and their children's religious and cultural needs, can be a somewhat elusive proposition.

One way these couples can achieve this objective is by adopting an approach that emphasizes what they hold in common when raising their children. The following remarks made by one non-Orthodox respondent who was raising his children in the Orthodox Church illustrate, this point. "We have determined to raise our children in the Orthodox Church. So, we tell them that they are Greek Orthodox Christians, but we also frequently just tell them that they are Christians. And it's not that we try and water down their Orthodox affiliation, but we find it easier to co-exist in a mixed Christian home if we emphasize both the Greek Orthodox and Christian dimension of their religious identity."

As this comment suggests, intermarried parents may try to strike a balance between what they hold in common with one another, and to de-emphasize what differences may exist between their religious traditions. One of the main reasons why such an approach is preferred by these couples is that it permits their children to remain respectful to both parents' religious traditions, as well as both grandparents' religious and cultural traditions. "We don't have to worry," stated another respondent, "about insulting the grandparents when we emphasize the fact that we are all Christians. This really makes it easier on everyone, because everyone feels more a part of each other and no one's feelings are hurt. Besides this, we believe that religion should not separate families but bring them together. And we also believe that's what God wants."

According to respondents, when intermarried parents adopt and utilize this approach, their marital and family life is enhanced, but when only one spouse's religious and cultural preferences are respected and valued, some degree of family instability is generally created. "I really had to learn this the hard way," stated one Greek Orthodox woman. "My church and parents taught me that Greek Orthodoxy is the one true faith, and I was insisting that our children receive this message... but it caused so much tension between my husband and me that I have mellowed considerably on this point. The way I look at it, God does not want us to be an unhappy couple and family... so, I have learned to be more tolerant and more respectful of my husband's religion and he is more respectful to me and my efforts to raise our children Orthodox. Therefore, we have compromised. We have agreed to tell our children that we are both Christians, but that they are also Orthodox Christians."

Naming the Children

When thinking about having children, some couples struggle with the Greek tradition that necessitates parents to name their first born after the Greek Orthodox spouse's parent. Reflecting back to a disagreement that one couple had over this, one non-Orthodox spouse stated: "It was kind of a shock to me when Jim told me he wanted to name our son "Eustratios," after his father. I found the whole tradition of naming the son after the father's father rather strange and intrusive. And worse than this, I also suddenly found myself caught between insulting my father-in-law and disappointing my husband and naming my baby a name I wasn't real crazy about."

Depending on each spouse's cultural/ethnic attachments, this decision may or may not be particularly challenging. For example, when both spouses have an essentially Americanized[1] worldview, intermarried couples will not find this tradition important nor feel obligated to follow it. In other instances, if one of the spouses has a strong attachment to his or her cultural/ethnic background, this spouse will generally determine whose ethnic traditions may impact how the children are named.

Furthermore, when the Greek Orthodox spouse is the one with strong ties to his or her ethnic background, then the couple may be challenged when selecting a name for their first-born. In some instances, such couples will determine to give their child two names, a legal name and the Greek grandparent's name at baptism. One non-Greek Orthodox respondent states, "I didn't have any problem giving my son his *Papou's* name at baptism, which was Athanasios, but I just couldn't consent to this when it came to his legal name."

In other instances, couples simply determined to give their first-born (especially the male first-born) his Greek Orthodox grandparent's first name. In this case the decision was made out of strong needs that existed from both the Greek Orthodox spouse, and his desire to honor his extended family. The following reflections typify this point. "Hey, my dad worked hard to raise me. He sacrificed everything to make certain that I got a good education… and you know, he didn't care about having a big house, a fine car… but having my first-born named after him meant everything to him…. How could I not do this for him? It was the right thing to do."

Baptizing the Children

While inter-Christian couples appear to respect and tolerate each other's religious preferences, they report engaging in more discussion and debate regarding their children's religious and spiritual development. A second challenge that some of these couples reported grappling with is where to baptize their children. "It wasn't so hard for us to accept and respect each other's religious background," stated one respondent while reflecting back to the couple's efforts to decide where to baptize their children, "but it was entirely another matter when it came to our children's baptism. So, we struggled a little more than usual over this decision."

While the decision to baptize was not especially troublesome for all these couples, it did create a moderate to high challenge for some. One chief reason this decision challenged some of these couples was linked to the notion that their children's baptism might determine where the family's future place of worship would be.

In an effort to decide where to baptize, numerous couples stated that honest, respectful communication was indispensable to them. For example, one respondent stated, "We sat down and looked at all the facts and we decided that since my wife would be spending more time with our kids, we should baptize them in her church." In addition, some couples reported that premarital discussions that concerned themselves with where their future children would be baptized and which names they would receive, proved beneficial to their family's religious well-being. The following statement was typical of what numerous respondents had to say about this point. "I told him before marriage that it didn't matter to me if he converted to the Greek Orthodox Church, but I couldn't accept my children being baptized in any other church than my own. And I don't know what would have happened to us if he resisted this request. That was really important to me, and I think he realized it."

Reasons Affecting the Parents' Decision to Baptize

It is also important to note that a decision regarding when and where inter-Christian couples' children are baptized is generally not made by accident. Certain factors appear to influence this decision with the following being of prominent importance.

First, when respondents appeared to have the same level of commitment to their religious tradition, one chief determining factor that helped many of these couples select the church where their future children would be baptized was based on gender.

Several respondents indicated that mothers are in a better position – due in large part to the greater amount of time they
spend with the children – to cultivate and nurture spirituality
in their children.

Second, when one spouse had a stronger faith than the other
did, participants' observations indicated that the spouse with
the strongest faith attachment had the greatest impact on where
their children were baptized. "It was clear from the beginning,"
stated one respondent. "My husband had the strongest attachment to his church and so the logical place for us to baptize
was in the Greek Church."

Third, it was also observed that non-Orthodox will respond
positively to the notion of baptizing their future children in the
Orthodox Church if they have some understanding and respect
for its theology and traditions. The following remarks made by
one non-Orthodox illustrate this point. "It wasn't that I was
against having my kids baptized in the Greek Church, but I
wanted to make sure that it was a Christian Church that would
teach my kids Christian ways. When I figured this out, there
was no real problem for me." Furthermore, some opposition
may occur if non-Orthodox are not completely convinced that
their future children will receive adequate Christian training,
or similar Christian teachings as they did when they were children. While commenting on the Sunday School program in the
Greek Orthodox Church his children were attending, one respondent made the following statement: "I'm not really thrilled
with the Sunday School at the Greek Church where my children go. It seems that there's no real substance to it. Sometimes
I feel that they are only learning how to color, and that's not
good enough. So, we've been talking about this, and I know it
upsets my wife, but I want them to know Christ, and if the
Greek Church can't help, then we've got to do something about
this. It may be that some religious home schooling could help."

Fourth, while extended family pressures were not mentioned
as being of primary importance, they were mentioned as play-

ing a secondary role of importance in a couple's decision to choose a church in which to baptize their children. In these instances, nuclear family needs were generally of primary importance while extended family needs (while important) were generally deemed of secondary importance. Moreover, when couples were unable to keep these priorities in order, they reported difficulties until such time as they were able to give primary importance to their nuclear family needs. In the words of one respondent who struggled with this issue, "Until I was able to say, 'Hey… I love you Mom and Dad, and you're important, but my family's needs have to come first…' my wife and I continued to have problems over this baptism thing." One couple that had a particularly difficult time in pleasing both sides of their extended family determined that it was going to be impossible to do so. In this case, the couple made a decision to baptize their children in the Greek Orthodox Church, and then respectfully suggested to everyone that only "those who are able to celebrate this event with them were invited, and all others should stay home."

The "Odd Person Out"

When the inter-Christian couples interviewed determined to baptize their children in the Greek Orthodox Church, they reported struggling to help the non-Orthodox partner to avoid "feeling like the odd person out" when it came to the family's religious life. As one father stated, "I can still remember the first time my four-year-old referred to Daddy's church and the rest of the family's church. It made me feel really left out and somewhat separated from him. And even though I try to be part of my kids' religious development, when they receive communion and I don't, it's a poignant reminder of the distance that exists between us in this area of their lives." In these instances spouses admitted that it was essentially unavoidable for the non-Orthodox parent to feel somewhat alienated and out of place in this area of the family's life. They also stated that an acknowledgment of these feelings by either one or both spouses helped minimize these feelings and also curtailed any destructive resentment that might build from these feelings. As one respondent stated, "My husband and I talk about it when I get bummed, and that makes me feel better. But it still hurts, and maybe one day I will opt to convert, but not now."

When Parents Disagree
When reflecting upon parents' efforts to make decisions about their children's religious development, participants observed that overt and/or covert squabbling and manipulation by one or both spouses was viewed as inappropriate and ultimately unhealthy for both the marriage and their children. Some spouses also indicated that when honest, open conversation regarding their children's religious needs had not occurred, they tended to struggle with ambivalent feelings. This was especially the case when one or both spouses felt that a mutually satisfying agreement regarding their children's religious development failed to materialize. In these cases, parents stated that they desired their children to experience many of the same religious experiences they had experienced as children and, "regretted giving in to certain pressures before marriage from their spouse and his or her extended family that prevent this from occurring." For example, one Catholic mother who had begrudgingly agreed to baptize her children in the Greek Orthodox Church stated the following: "I wanted my daughter to have her First Communion and Confirmation. And it really disappointed me to realize she would not experience what I experienced." An undercurrent of tension often pervaded these couples' discussions when the topic of religion was broached. This was due in part to spouses' failure to arrive at mutually agreeable resolutions about their children's religious development before or after marriage.

Couples also stated that a failure to amicably decide where their children would be baptized and receive their religious training could potentially jeopardize their children's religious development. For example, while considering the difficulties that one couple had encountered over the years regarding their children's religious training, one respondent made the following observations: "We've struggled over our children's religious upbringing for years. And I guess we never really came to any resolution. So maybe that's why some of our children are indifferent to religion and several don't even belong to a church."

Several participants maintained that children reared in a home that is conflicted over religion might negatively impact their children's perception of religion, and even cause some children to avoid religion altogether as adults. Along these same lines, these couples also believed that if their children belonged to one church, the children's confusion about religion would be minimized and religious and spiritual development would be facilitated. Choosing a church and then agreeing to raise their children (with consistency) in this faith tradition were deemed important to their children's religious development. "Children need structure, and that applies to their religious training. We made the decision early on to bring them up in one church, and this has made a world of difference to their religious development. I'm sure they would not be as attached to their religion if we sent them to both churches."

Living in a Multicultural Society

Although most of these couples were raising their children in the Orthodox Church, many indicated that they did not want their children to develop a parochial, exclusionary perspective of the world. To illustrate this, consider the following comment: "As I listen to the group's conversation about children, I'm starting to worry a little more. My son, who was baptized in the Greek Orthodox Church, has grown up in a sterile environment because he has come to this Church, which is primarily Greek. And it's all he sees, and I worry a bit about that. I want him to be exposed to many different types of people. I prefer to see an emphasis on a multinational environment. And even though I'm proud that he's half-Greek, I don't want my kids to develop a culturally narrow view of the world."

Many of these respondents' observations appeared to suggest that they viewed this as a challenge and encouraged their children to develop a respect for (a) their Greek Orthodox heritage, (b) the non-Orthodox partner's religious and cultural heritage, and (c) all religions and cultures. For example, one respondent stated, "My kids went to a Jewish preschool because I want them to be well-rounded, tolerant, and understanding of difference. I believe we have to try to get along with everyone. So I hope my kids would never think to say anything about their friends who are Jewish. And even more than this, I continue to ask my husband to teach me all he knows about his Polish culture so that I can teach our kids. I want them to know about others and I want them to know about their Greek and Polish backgrounds."

Despite parents' best efforts to raise their children in one church, however, many participants also stated that they believed that their children would acquire a more inclusive perception of Christianity by virtue of living in an inter-Christian household. In an effort to address this latter point one respondent stated, "Even though they come to the Greek Church, there is no doubt in my mind that our children will grow up with a predominantly American viewpoint, and be exposed to a lot of different influences. And I also think that they will have a Christian way of looking at the world, not just simply a Greek Orthodox way."

Along these same lines, many of these parents also recognized that they lived in a multicultural, multi-religious society, and that it was moderately to highly probable that their children might not continue to worship in the church where they were baptized and were presently being raised. One participant's remarks appear to summarize most respondents'

sentiments regarding this latter point. "As hard as I try to in-
still a basic pride in my kids for their background, I also know
that there may be a chance that they will marry outside of the
Greek Orthodox Church. After all, we live in a society where
there are many types of people. So, if my children fall in love
with a non-Greek, I can't say to them, 'Leave the house.' No. I
will say, 'Let's consider how you can get married in the Greek
Church.' However, if they don't want that, well, then I will have
to accept that and support them as best as I can.... I won't be
happy, but I'll support them."

Numerous comments also suggested that these participants
would be considerably more unsettled if their children chose
to embrace a non-Christian religious tradition. The following
remarks were indicative of how many parents felt. "I am trying to raise them in the Greek Church, but there are many religions in this country, and once they are old enough, I suppose
there's a chance they may jump ship and change. In addition,
while this might bother me, it won't bother too much if they
change to another Christian religion. If they were to choose a
non-Christian religion, well that's a different story entirely. That
would probably bother me a lot more." In relation to these latter concerns, participants stated that they felt that the religious
and cultural differences would likely prove to be destructive
to the marriage and, also ultimately jeopardize their
grandchildren's religious and cultural identity. While reflecting on these observations, one respondent added: "I mean, how
can children really learn who they are if their parents' religious
backgrounds are too different? The radical cultural and religious differences will only serve to confuse them and deny them
an opportunity to develop a religious and cultural identity."

Explaining Intermarriage to the Children

Intermarried couples report experiencing some apprehen-
sion and concern when trying to explain their religious differences to their children. This may be the case because they want

their children to grow up respecting both parents' faith traditions while also acquiring a healthy religious identity. These two objectives may not be "mutually exclusive, but they..." may at times contradict one another. For example, these parents recognize that when they are respectful to both spouses' traditions, this may result in diluting their children's efforts to bond with one religious tradition which could in turn have a negative impact on their children's sense of religious identity. Trying to strike a balance between being respectful to both religious traditions and raising their children in one religious tradition can and does pose some challenges for these families.

Some couples described moderate levels of discomfort when they attempted to explain their religious differences to their maturing children. They stated that they were often unable to answer these types of questions and felt intimidated by them. One typical question mentioned was: "Why can't Mommy and Daddy receive communion together in the Orthodox Church?" Another similar question was: "Why do we celebrate Easter on two different days?" In many cases participants stated that they gave age-appropriate responses. Some also stated that they waited until they could talk with their priest before giving a complete answer. Furthermore, many parents tended to believe that a complete answer had a positive impact on their children's efforts to develop a healthy perspective of religion and/or a religious identity.

The Religious Identity of the Children

Participants repeatedly indicated that parents should take a proactive approach in their children's religious development, but in many instances also admitted that they had frequently fallen short of this parental responsibility. Those who had assumed an active role in their children's religious development indicated that they had also profited from this endeavor. As one respondent stated, "I think that one of the reasons that many parents don't take an active role in their children's religious formation is because they don't know their Greek Orthodox faith. Moreover, I happen to be one of these types of parents. But one day I just decided that this needed to stop, and I ordered some books and began teaching myself and my children."

Inter-Christian couples that perceive themselves as successfully instilling their children with a religious identity have often done so by arriving at mutually agreeable decisions, and then offering religious training that is primarily consistent with one faith tradition. This means that while they understand that their children will likely be exposed to both parents' cultural and faith traditions, they work together to help them develop a respect for both faith traditions, but primarily raise them in one faith tradition. The recognition that their children will be indoctrinated into one faith tradition seems to be their preferred approach since many of these parents believe that doing otherwise will result in confusing their children and diluting their commitment to religion. As a way to illustrate this, consider the following short exchange that occurred in one group between two parents.

> Husband: "We realized early on that we couldn't raise them in both churches because that seemed to be religious suicide."
> Wife: "That's right, I mean we didn't want to kill their efforts at developing a religious identity."
> Husband: "The kids needed consistency and structure."
> Wife: "And without them, we were afraid they'd have nothing to build on."
> Husband: "That pretty much says it all."

Help from the Church

In a world that is filled with numerous threats to their children's emotional, moral, spiritual and physical well-being, these couples stated that they turned to the Church to receive support in their efforts to help their children acquire a Christian world view. Couples stated that their busy schedules and the increasingly secular society they live in present problems for them in their efforts to indoctrinate their children in the faith. "We've started going to church more," stated one respondent, "because we are concerned that our kids won't get an adequate moral foundation. If you don't have this foundation, what kind of a person will you eventually be?"

Intergenerational Differences
Participants also stated that they would try to use less guilt, manipulation and other similar controlling strategies in their efforts to indoctrinate their children into the faith. "When I stopped going to church at around age 19, my mother tried to make me feel guilty. However, all that did was push me further away from the church. Like the old saying goes, I think you can catch more flies with honey than you can with vinegar." Another respondent stated, "As a parent, guilt can take you just so far when it comes to helping your children acquire a religious identity. My background is full of attempts to make me feel guilty about any number of things related to religion. Moreover, I honestly think that all the guilt and manipulation pushed me away from the religion. It wasn't until a few years before our children arrived when I had a religious experience that helped me see religion from a healthier perspective. That experience convinced me that guilt and manipulation have little or no place in a parent's efforts to help their children learn the value of religion."

Boundary Issues
Negotiating clear, healthy boundaries that respect each parent's sensitivities and preferences regarding their children's religious and spiritual development was repeatedly mentioned as important. When parents were not in agreement about their children's religious training, this negatively impacted their children's religious development and created a source of family stress. To make this point one respondent stated, "We realized the hard way that our constant bickering about the kids' religious upbringing didn't help them. One day, while we were arguing about something, our oldest daughter said, 'When I grow up I'm not going to church. It's not worth it.' And when

she said that, I realized that we needed to stop the arguing and get together on this religion thing or our kids would either grow up without a religion or change to a different religion."

Couples also recognized the importance of drawing healthy boundaries between themselves and their children. To be more specific, participants generally believed that children lack the maturity to make well-informed decisions about their religious development, and parents must be part of this decision well into their children's young adult lives especially if a child appears to show an interest in a questionable religious sect.

Participants also identified the need to draw certain clear boundaries between their own nuclear family and their families of origin when making decisions about their children's religious development. They believed that most intermarried couples have to contend with extended family intrusions when it comes to their children's religious development. It was deemed to be very important to inform grandparents that the parents have been entrusted with making decisions about the religious development of their children, and that grandparents should assume the role of consultants and only offer solicited advice. The grandparents' conflicting religious traditions and unsolicited advice could undermine and create unhealthy alliances that would compromise their children's spiritual development. In one instance, a respondent reported experiencing some conflict with his mother-in-law over religion. His concern was that his child might one day choose to worship in "grandma's church" because of her continued meddling in their children's religious development.

Church Attendance by Children

Participating couples wanted their children to have a religious experience that was similar to their own. They repeatedly reported that having children motivated many of them to regularize the frequency of their church attendance, as individuals and as a family. Parents perceived that regular family

attendance is important to their children's religious development, and that family worship reduces the likelihood that their
children will become confused about religious matters. Children also compelled the parents to develop a more sophisti-
cated understanding of their own religion which in some cases
facilitated a deeper spiritual relationship between individual
spouses and God and between both spouses and God.

Viewing Challenges in Positive Terms

While there are many potential problems that confront intermarried couples in their efforts to facilitate their children's
religious development, this observation does not imply that
these challenges are insurmountable, or that they impact their
children's religious development negatively. Most intermarried
couples suggested that it is possible to negotiate their religious
differences effectively, and to raise religiously and spiritually
committed children. They did not view their decision to enter
into an inter-Christian intercultural marriage as a liability that
might impoverish or compromise their children's religious and
spiritual development. On the contrary, intermarried couples
generally asserted that with God's help, their intercultural and
inter-Christian marriages enriched their children's religious and
cultural well-being.

Summary

Participants indicated that premarital discussions relating to
their future children's baptism and developing religious identity were important. Such discussions appeared to avert serious disagreements after marriage.

Couples who chose to raise their children in the Greek Orthodox Church also tried to help them develop an Orthodox
Christian identity. By proceeding in this manner, both spouses
felt somewhat connected to their children's religious development. Moreover, such an approach appeared to have a positive
impact on their children's religious development.

If couples failed to discuss certain issues before marriage, these issues invariably surfaced after marriage. Challenges related to (a) children's names, (b) the church where the children would be baptized, and (c) how to keep the non-Orthodox partner from feeling left out from his/her children's religious development required some time and attention.

Children's inter-Christian questions challenged many parents. This was because parents felt committed to providing answers that respected their children's developing religious identity and both partners' religious traditions. Such answers were difficult to formulate.

Finding ways of working productively through disagreements that were related to their children's religious and cultural development also challenged parents. Discussions that led to constructive conclusions appeared to impact their children's developing religious identity in positive ways.

Chapter Seven

Honor your father and mother, that your days may be long in the land which the Lord your God gives you. – *Ex.20:12*

The love of husband and wife is the force that welds society together. – *St. John Chrysostom*

The age of focus groups' participants generally determined the quality and extent of conversation that took place about extended families. Generation Xers (ages 20-34) spent more time discussing extended family issues and challenges. This presumably was the case because Xers are still trying to work through extended family issues. In contrast, Baby Boomers (ages 35-52) have likely negotiated and formed healthy boundaries between themselves and their extended families. Baby Boomers were not, however, immune to experiencing extended family challenges. The frequency and degree of these challenges were fewer and less intense or somehow connected to failed attempts to resolve extended family challenges early on in their marriages. This chapter will discuss some of the common extended family challenges that intermarried couples may encounter during the dating process and over the first few years of marriage. Knowledge of what young couples can expect, together with an awareness that other couples have experienced similar challenges, can assist them in their efforts to negotiate healthy resolutions to the extended family challenges they may face.

Dating and the Adjustment Period After Marriage

Many participants' comments inferred that their parents' approval and happiness with their choice of dating partners was important to them, and they tried to date individuals who would please their parents. While participants generally tried to find a spouse that would please their parents/extended families, sometimes they were not successful. In these instances, participants described being caught between their desire to please their parents and their growing love and affection for their dating partner. Typical remarks that were made regarding this point were as follows: "My parents' approval was important. I really wanted them to like him, and I didn't know what might happen if they didn't care for him, since I had fallen head-over-heels in love with him. The fact that he wasn't Greek made me kind of nervous."

Parents' blessings and approval were not always immediately forthcoming. Many participants described experiencing some initial displeasure from their parents during the dating process and subsequent engagement that created tensions between the dating couple, and one or both extended families. "Both of my parents wanted me to marry a Greek man, and that's what it seems I heard every single day when I got old enough to date. Therefore, when I started dating someone who was not Greek, the pressure increased, and it affected us for a while. It got so bad that at one point Sam refused to come to my parent's home when we were dating. I'm sure that didn't bother my parents at the time, but it sure bothered me. It made things really awkward between us all. Fortunately this awkward period didn't last. We all get along super now. Sometimes I even think they love Sam more than me."

A few participants also reported that ill feelings lingered into the first few years of marriage because their extended families had not entirely accepted their inter-Christian intercultural marriage. This was especially true of many – but certainly not all – Greek Orthodox participants' experiences. Some also reported temporary and extended-family cut-offs that occurred because of continued extended-family displeasure. The following observations illustrate this. "I came from Greece and I knew that my parents would object to me marrying a non-Greek. So, I bypassed them, and in the process created friction between them and us. So much so, that for a while we didn't have any contact because they wouldn't accept my wife. But now, at least, we talk and I have been back to see them. But my wife still resents them, and only goes with me because she knows it pleases me."

Couples' comments indicated that the length of time that their parents had spent in this country seemed to influence their reaction to their choice of dating partners and subsequent marriage. Immigrant families and extended families that had only been in this country for one or two generations were more likely to have stronger ties to the mother country and thus offered more resistance to dating couples. This resistance was especially prominent as the relationship became more serious. In making this point, one respondent stated, "Hey, what do you expect? My parents are from Greece and they always wanted me to marry within the culture. Being Greek is important to my family... the thought of my marrying a non-Greek really upset them at first... but they got over it once they got to know her." In another group, a non-Greek respondent stated, "My mother is a traditional Puerto Rican woman, and when I told her that I was marrying a Greek man, she had some initial concerns that even lingered for some time after we got married."

In relation to this point, because most Greek Orthodox extended families are relative newcomers to this country when compared to their non-Greek extended family counterparts, couples experiencing extended family resistance were generally referring to the Greek Orthodox extended family. Many Greek Orthodox parents were described as valuing and encouraging single-church and single-culture marriages. "My parents are from Greece," stated one respondent, "so their initial disapproval was predictable. My wife's parents have been in this country almost since the pilgrims arrived, so they didn't care so long as she was marrying someone who was Christian." In addition to parental pressure, pressure from Greek Orthodox grandparents was also repeatedly mentioned. In the words of one respondent, "Sure it's true that my parents gave me some grief over dating a non-Greek, but don't forget about *Yiayia*[1] pressure. This kind of pressure can be even more pronounced than parental pressure." Big brother pressure was also another prominent type of pressure alluded to by some respondents. "Since my father died a few years ago, my brother has sort of looked after me and assumed his role. So, when he found out that I was thinking about marrying a non-Greek, he started acting like my father. It was at that point that I had to remind him I loved him, but he was my brother and I needed to make my own decisions about marriage. This didn't please him, but we eventually reached an understanding."

Conversely, families that had been in this country for a longer period of time were generally described as being less resistant to the notion of their son or daughter dating someone from a different ethnic and/or Christian background. Parents with a more "Americanized" perspective had lower parental expectations regarding inter-ethnic and inter-Christian marriages. Both the level of an extended family's ethnicity and the length of time that each spouse's family of origin had been in this country were directly associated with the amount of resistance and discouragement inter-Christian dating couples encountered.

Some participants whose parents were both "very religious" and from Greece seemed to offer less resistance to their adult children when they entered a serious, inter-Christian, inter-cultural dating situation. One respondent stated, "My parents, who are immigrants, never forced me to marry someone Greek. Certainly, they would not have objected to my marrying a Greek – I believe they would have preferred this – but they were more interested in whether he was Christian and had a good Christian heart. They are very religious people and it was more important to them that my husband be Christian rather than Greek."

When Greek Orthodox family members exerted pressure on their adult child to cool their involvement with their non-Orthodox dating partner, this tended to both confuse and insult some non-Orthodox who had been raised in families who had a low nominal ethnic identity. Several non-Orthodox stated that they were not only confused by these attitudes toward non-Greeks, but also interpreted such attitudes as insulting and myopic in character.

Some non-Orthodox extended families were also described as valuing inter-Christian marriage as opposed to single-church and single cultural marriage, and desired that their adult child marry a Christian rather than someone from the same ethnic and faith tradition. One possible exception to this was non-Orthodox extended families belonging to religious groups that have a fundamentalist, exclusive view of religion. In these instances, inter-Christian couples received high amounts of pressure from one or both parents belonging to these types of non-Orthodox religious groups. "My Mom is a strong believer," stated one non-Orthodox participant. "She belongs to a church that has some very conservative views. I mean, they believe that if you're not part of their church, you're not going to heaven. So, when she heard that I was considering marriage to a Greek Orthodox Christian she made things pretty difficult for us because she didn't hide her beliefs and disapproval. It's a little better now, but there's still a lot of tension in the air if the subject of religion comes up."

Finally, extended families that viewed inter-Christian dating and intermarriage from a positive perspective tended to have a positive effect on the dating process, engagement, and marriage. Positive extended family support was also construed as having a beneficial effect on couples' relationships with their parents and on family togetherness.

Pressures to Wed in the Greek Orthodox Church

The Orthodox Church's pastoral guidelines can also create challenges for couples. "The Orthodox Church has certain rules about where an Orthodox can get married," stated one participant. "If I were to get married outside of the Orthodox Church, I would no longer be in good standing. So to satisfy this requirement, we decided to marry in the Orthodox Church. Besides, it was really no big sacrifice. We both loved the service, and so did everyone who attended."

Greek Orthodox parents can also exert a great deal of pressure on couples when they are deciding on where the wedding will take place. Some parents will make it known that they will offer their blessings as long as the couple agrees to marry in the Orthodox Church. As a result of the Orthodox Church's rules, together with Greek Orthodox parent's pressure, couples will generally determine to marry in the Orthodox Church. However, getting to this point is not always easy. Sometimes couples encounter some challenges.

Participants' comments suggested that some Greek Orthodox grandparents and parents tended to utilize excessive amounts of guilt and manipulation to convince the couples to get married and attend the Greek Orthodox Church after marriage. For example, in talking about his grandmother, one respondent stated, "She started appealing to my conscience saying things like, 'this was your grandfather's church, how can you think about going anywhere else,' and 'what would he say if he were alive today.' Well, I knew what he would say, he would say that I needed to get married in my family's Church, and that made me feel real bad." These pressures tended to make the Greek Orthodox partner feel uncomfortable because as one participant stated, "I began to feel as if I was caught between trying to please my family and my fiancée."

In addition, if the Orthodox dating partner buckles under extended family pressure, and tries to convince his/her non-Orthodox spouse to get married in the Greek Orthodox Church;

the non-Orthodox fiancée may feel both hurt and betrayed if he/she realizes what is happening. "He actually talked to his mother about our marriage taking place in the Greek Church before he talked to me. And that really hurt. I felt like, hey, this is my marriage, not hers. What business is it of hers until we've discussed it." In addition, Greek Orthodox spouses generally reported feeling guilty about siding with their family-of-origin, and then angry at their family for introducing premarital strife into the premarital process. While responding to this statement, the husband said, "Yes, she was right. I should have talked to her first. I was dead wrong... and later I thought about how my mother kind of cornered me into this discussion and I was kind of angry with her. But it taught me an important lesson - never discuss things with your parents before you've discussed them with your spouse."

Finding ways of meeting the couples' needs, while also meeting extended family needs, will not be easy, but is possible. Generally, time, prayer, and honest respectful conversation help, as can a discussion with the priest.

Pressure Lessens Before Marriage

Once it seemed apparent that a couple had decided to get married, almost all extended families appeared to soften, and were considerably more supportive, especially if a couple consented to worship in the Greek Orthodox Church. "It was just a matter of telling them," stated one respondent, "that we would be praying in the Greek Church, and that dissolved the tension and pressure among all of us."

This does not suggest that extended family challenges end at this point because many extended families require more time to warm up to someone from another religious and/or cultural/ ethnic background. Consider the following quote from one participant. "Don't misunderstand, my family really loves my husband, but it wasn't always like this. For some time after the marriage, things were somewhat unsteady between him and my family. But things are better now that we all figured out some stuff, and arrived at an understanding… he became so much a part of us, that sometimes I think he's closer to my parents than I am."

Time, respect and an open-minded attitude on the part of all concerned are usually important as couples and extended families seek to coalesce and make the needed adjustments before the marriage takes place. If an engaged couple is experiencing family pressure before they wed, they should try to remember that most of these pressures will lift as they seek to meet their needs and the extended families' needs before the Sacrament of Marriage is celebrated.

After the Honeymoon and Greek Orthodox Extended Families
While Greek Orthodox parents may experience some initial disappointment when their son or daughter informs them that they intend to marry a non-Greek Orthodox Christian, this disappointment eventually fades. One of the initial factors responsible for changing parents' attitudes and feelings is connected to the Greek Orthodox parents' desire that their child be happy. As one respondent stated, "I knew that my parents weren't happy with my decision, but they eventually supported me because they wanted me to be happy." Another factor is connected to a couple's decision to worship in the Greek Orthodox Church. "The fact that most of my brothers and sisters got married in the Greek Orthodox Church," stated one respondent, "even though our marriages were inter-Christian, pleased my mother. And in some ways that was enough." Fears that the parental displeasure might alienate the couple also motivated some Greek parents to respect and accept the inter-Christian couple's decision. One respondent stated, "I know my parents wondered what the consequences might be if they didn't accept our decision to get married. Would I stop speaking to them for a period of time, would we never speak… were running through their minds because I was determined to marry my

wife." In addition, once parents and grandparents discerned that their child/grandchild had found happiness with their non-Greek Orthodox mate, they also tended to accept these inter-Christian intercultural unions. "When I look back at the flack that we received in an effort to get married, I now realize that all my parents really only wanted was for me to be happy. Once they saw that I was happy, things changed and they accepted my wife, Sharon, with open arms," related one participant.

Additional factors that seemed to change Greek Orthodox parents' attitudes were their child's efforts to follow some of the Greek traditions and their child's non-Orthodox mate's willingness to respect and learn about Greek Orthodoxy. While discussing these, one respondent said the following about his parents, "Once they saw that I wasn't going to leave the church or stop being Greek, my folks seemed to come around. And once they also saw that Jack was interested and respectful in what we believed, this made it even better between us all."

Time and the arrival of children also appear to minimize the amount of disapproval some intermarried couples experience from extended Greek Orthodox family members. Time and grandchildren also tend to enhance intimacy between (a) the non-Greek Orthodox partner and extended families, and (b) between nuclear families and extended families. This is especially true when intermarried couples choose to raise their children in the Greek Orthodox Church. While describing the tension that existed between him and his Greek Orthodox in-laws, one respondent stated, "They couldn't be angry at me for marrying their daughter any longer when we decided to raise our kids in the Greek Orthodox church.... From then on, I've been treated like a prince." These family dynamics also occurred between intermarried couples and non-Orthodox extended families, but with less frequency.

After the Honeymoon and the Non-Orthodox Partner

Comments suggested that some extended families tried to make couples feel guilty because they had either chosen to remain in an inter-Christian marriage, or because their choice-of-worship communities was different than their own. In most instances, participants stated that when compared to non-Orthodox extended families, Greek Orthodox families tended to be more hypersensitive to the couple's efforts to choose a worship site. Specifically, Greek Orthodox families tended to apply more pressure on inter-Christian couples to attend the Orthodox Church, and were generally described as being more distressed if a couple chose to worship outside of the Orthodox Church. Reflecting back on how his in-laws reacted when he and his wife left the Greek Church, one participant stated, "When we decided to try the Presbyterian Church, my wife's parents were really distressed. Her father even took me aside and asked me about this church and what they taught. He was not pleased with our decision and told me so. It took things a long time to settle between her parents and us. And it really wasn't until we decided to return to the Greek Church that things started normalizing between us all. I now attend my church, and periodically also attend the Greek Church. This seems suitable to all concerned."

Non-Orthodox Extended Family Reactions to the Orthodox Church

While there were certainly some exceptions, non-Orthodox extended families were essentially described as being content if the couple was simply attending a Christian Church, and were not unsettled if the couple chose to attend the Greek Orthodox Church on a frequent basis. When couples were asked to account for this disparity, several stated that they thought most non-Orthodox extended families appeared to be satisfied if their son or daughter choose to attend a Christian Church, whereas Greek Orthodox extended families were inclined to be displeased unless the couple selected a Greek Orthodox parish.

If a couple chose to attend the Greek Orthodox Church on a regular basis, numerous participants observed that the religious and ethnic exclusivity frequently served to create tension between them and the non-Orthodox partner's extended family. Participants noted that non-Orthodox extended family members described feeling especially disconcerted with the Orthodox Church's rules regarding their participation in the sacraments. "My in-laws are still confused about the Orthodox Church's rules, and how they excluded them during our wedding and the baptism of our two children," stated one respondent. "And I don't think their attitude will change anytime soon." To be more specific, several participants described hurt feelings that non-Orthodox extended family members felt when they were informed they could not function as a sponsor during the wedding or as a godparent. While the strategy was not always effective in addressing hurt feelings, it seems that when the Orthodox partner could respectfully articulate the Orthodox Church's position regarding non-Orthodox participation, hurt feelings were lessened. When the Orthodox partner was unable to offer a clear justification for the Orthodox Church's position, the hurt feelings were exacerbated. "I really think if I knew my faith better, some of the hard feelings that developed when we were selecting a godparent would not have occurred. I just didn't know how to tell my brother-in-law he couldn't assume this role without sounding really crass. If I knew what I know now, I think could have deflected many of the misunderstandings that developed."

Drawing Clear Boundaries

Participants repeatedly stated that it was necessary to learn how to draw healthy boundaries between themselves and their extended families in order to protect their families from unwanted intrusions. Consider the following observations made by one respondent. "Early on in our marriage, I felt like I was caught between what my wife wanted and what my parents wanted. On the one hand, my wife wanted us to worship in the Orthodox Church, but my parents wanted me to worship in the Catholic Church. Well, I can't tell you how uncomfortable that made me feel because I felt stuck between these two strong pulls. But I got through it okay once I realigned my priorities and put my marriage first. After that I considered my parent's desires and needs, but never put them on a equal footing with my wife's and family's needs."

Participants also repeatedly observed that when intermarried couples were unsuccessful in drawing clear boundaries between themselves and their extended families, some respondents were forced to subordinate and/or ignore their nuclear family needs in an effort to meet extended families' expectations and needs. One respondent stated, "We had to do the marriage thing in both churches to please both sides of our families." In another group, another participant stated, "We ended up baptizing some of our children in the Greek Orthodox Church, and some in the in-laws' church to make everyone happy. The only problem with that is it didn't make us and our children happy, and we regret that decision now."

Summary

Generally speaking, intermarried couples experience most extended family challenges while they are dating and during the first five to eight years of marriage. Most adult children try to choose dating partners that will please their parents. This is not always possible. When adult children fall in love and determine to marry individuals who do not share their religious and cultural background, such decisions can distress their parents. These disagreements can linger well after marriage, creating tension between (a) both spouses, and (b) one or both spouses and extended family members.

Finding ways to reduce tension is imperative, since such tension can have a negative effect on marital and family satisfaction. In most instances, couples must learn to draw clear boundaries between themselves and extended family. Time, prayer and patience can also greatly assist couples in their efforts to negotiate and resolve extended family challenges.

Dominant American Culture

Faith Communities

Extended Families

Interfaith Families

Interfaith
Marriages

Individual
Spouses

Time

An Orthodox Social Ecological Developmental Theory

Chapter Eight

Acquiring a Better Understanding of Unique Challenges Faced By Intermarried Couples

Be subject to one another out of reverence for Christ –
Eph.5:21.

The preceding diagram provides a visual picture of the main human systems that effect intermarried couples. The smallest circle at the center of this diagram suggests that intermarried spouses are part of an inter-Christian marriage. This scheme also indicates that inter-Christian, intercultural marriages are part of an inter-Christian family, and these families are part of at least two extended family systems.[1] This diagram also illustrates how intermarried spouses, their marriages, families, as well as their extended families are generally couched within two faith communities, and that these faith communities are embedded in our dominant American culture.

What is not as evident from an examination of this diagram, however, is that intermarried spouses have certain needs, as do their marriages, families, extended families, and the faith communities to which they belong. Moreover, in a perfect world where everything lines up and fits together, all these needs would fit together perfectly. In an imperfect world like the one that we live in, these needs do not always fit together perfectly, but conflict with each other. In consequence, intermarried spouses and couples are constantly seeking to bring these conflicting subsystem needs into some balance. One respondent stated, "Everyone wants to be content and happy. In order to achieve this, married people have to be concerned with more than their own interests and needs. They also have to concern themselves with what their partner is thinking and wanting, what their children need, and what their parents expect. It's a real juggling act that requires some learned skills."

The materials that follow will begin listing the principal subsystem needs that IRP respondents identified. Examples of how the various subsystem needs conflict with each will also be given. It is hoped that this information – together with the information in chapter seven, will begin to help couples understand some of the reasons why intermarried couples experience challenges.

Principal Individual Needs

Participants repeatedly alluded to certain personal religious and spiritual needs that their various faith traditions met. Many stated that they could not imagine themselves attending any other church because of their moderate to high attachment to their religious and cultural background. Some typical responses were as follows, "Being a Mexican Catholic is a big part of what I am. It's part of me, and I couldn't ever give it up. I explored other religions, but eventually made a full circle and came back to what felt familiar and like home." Respondents inferred that their religious and spiritual needs were better met in the religious tradition they were familiar with as compared to other forms of Christianity. An Orthodox participant stated, "When I'm in church, and the incense is in the air, and Father Nick is chanting, and the icons are staring at me, I feel like I'm with God. I tried other churches, but they just didn't work for me. I think it's because the external stimuli that create a prayerful mood were missing."

Many respondents also observed that their religious background helped them and the members of their families live a moral existence. "I go to church," stated another participant, "because the church makes me a better person. You live in a dog-eat-dog world, and sometimes this affects your perspective on life. Coming to church gives me and my family the moral grounding we need." Respondents especially noted the positive moral impact religion had on their children. "Life is hard these days. I make it a point to bring our children to church because it teaches them right from wrong. By doing this, I feel like I'm fulfilling one of my obligations as a parent. Teaching my children to do the right thing is very important to me."

Respondents repeatedly mentioned how their faith was important to their sense of identity and psychological well-being. One respondent stated, "I don't know how non-religious people do it. My relationship with God is as important to me as any other relationship I have. Without His presence in my life, I don't know how happy and healthy I would be. You see, I'm an alcoholic who hasn't touched alcohol for fifteen years. But without God's help, I hesitate to imagine where I would be – probably in some bar drowning my sorrows." The following conversation also illustrates this point. During this exchange, two spouses are explaining the reason they are still an intermarried couple.

The husband, who is Greek Orthodox, speaks first. "Sometimes I think a little bit about going to her church, but then I think, maybe she'll convince me that this is okay, 'Jeez, the kids like it, you like it,' and eventually I lose that certain part of my identity. And how will this affect me?"

His wife responds, "Yeah. That's what he's so afraid of, losing that part of his identity, and he's so strict with the kids about that too, that that's their identity, being Greek."

He says, "No, I'm not."

She says, "Yes."

He says, "No."

She says again, "Yes, you do."

He replies, "Okay, maybe so."

Others pointed to the social benefits they derived from their religious background. In these cases, participants stated that membership in their religious background facilitated and maintained a connection with their familial ancestors, extended family, and with others who had a common religious and cultural experience. "I can't tell you all the reasons why I come," stated one respondent, "but it's got something to do with the fact that it was my *Papou's*[2] Church. My family goes there, and there are people there that I know." Another respondent stated, "I like being Greek. I like Greek food, Greek people, Greek traditions and speaking Greek. So, I come because other Greeks will be there and I can be Greek with them for about an hour each week. I guess it's good for me for that reason." In another group a respondent stated, "Being Church of Christ has mattered to the members of my family for generations. In fact, the church I belong to was essentially built by my grandfather. When I go there it's like going home. It feels like a big family reunion. And even though this sounds silly, sometimes I can even feel my granddad smiling down on me. He was a big influence in my life and continues to be a big influence."

Numerous participants also described a need to have their partners feel accepted and welcomed in their church. They often stated their attendance and support of their church was dependent on their spouses' level of comfort and interest. "I know this may sound kind of silly, but if I feel that if Sarah is welcomed and comfortable when we come to church, this makes me feel better, and I think I need this because it makes me feel more inclined to come back." In another focus group, the following similar comments were made. "Gloria has helped me develop an appreciation for my Greek Orthodox Church from her own example. She loves her faith and Puerto Rican heritage. She has been encouraging me to attend Liturgy more. One way she has done this is by attending with me. So I will tell you, if I perceived that she wasn't welcomed because she isn't Greek, I would never have grown so close to my Greek Orthodox Church over the years."

Many participants frequently alluded to an inherent need to see their children baptized in their church. This was especially true when respondents had high levels of ethnic and religious connections to their religious tradition. One respondent stated, "I didn't mind that we were going to be an inter-Christian couple, but I knew I couldn't accept our children being baptized in another church. This was so important to me that if he wasn't open to this before marriage, I honestly don't know if we would have gotten married."

As previously mentioned, many participants inferred that their parents' approval and happiness with their choice of partners was important to them, and they tried to select and date individuals that would please their parents. "I know this may sound kind of old fashioned in this day and age, but when I was dating, I looked for someone whom I liked, but I also sometimes considered my parents and family. When Hal and I began getting serious, I started wondering how my parents would feel about him because their opinions are important to me."

To summarize, according to the results from the IRP, participants indicated that their religious and cultural backgrounds served to meet certain personal needs. Some of these needs were religious, some were psychological, some were social, and some were closely interrelated to nuclear family and extended family needs. And while not all respondents described having identical needs, in varying degrees, most described a desire to remain attached to their religious tradition and ethnic backgrounds because these associations met certain personal needs that were important to their self-image and personal well-being.

Principal Couple Needs

All couples yearn for stability and marital satisfaction. Sometimes marital satisfaction and stability can be compromised as a result of a partner's differences. For example, different opinions over such things as the way couples will spend their money, the frequency of their lovemaking, how they will raise and parent their children, and the amount of household responsibilities each partner will assume can create serious disagreements that can adversely affect marital satisfaction and stability.

Because religion and ethnicity can have a profound impact on the way a person thinks, believes and behaves, religious and ethnic differences can potentially have a negative effect on marital satisfaction and stability. The following remarks make this point. "I was concerned about how Maria's Greek Orthodox background would ultimately affect me and our marriage. She has a strong affection for her background, as do I for my Methodist background. So I wondered how we were going to balance our personal religious and cultural needs and grow in our marriage."

Respondents stated that if they desired marital stability and satisfaction, they could not simply consider their own personal religious and cultural needs to the exclusion of their (partners') needs. They reported that as they were successful in striking a balance between their personal and marital needs, marital stability and satisfaction increased and their personal religious and cultural needs were satisfied. When spouses ignored their own needs, or their partner's needs, or their relationship's needs, then one or both spouses experienced some internal conflict which often translated into marital instability and dissatisfaction. The following two examples illustrate how couples can benefit from working though their personal and couple religious needs, or can have difficulties when they fail to reach a mutually satisfying balance between their personal and couple needs. The first couple engaged in a reasonably healthy process while the second couple exemplified what can go wrong when couples fail to strike a balance between their individual and couple needs.

Balancing Individual and Couple Needs

Tom and Katina have been married for two years. Tom has high levels of commitment to his Irish-Catholic background, and Katina has equally strong levels of commitment to her Greek Orthodox background. They also value family worship and do not want to worship separately on Sunday. Both talked about how they might reconcile their seemingly contradictory individual and couple needs. Over time, they decided that they will make the Greek Orthodox Church their primary place of worship and Tom will attend the Catholic Church on weekdays to receive the sacraments. In the event that Tom's family is celebrating a special family event in church, Katina will attend the Catholic Church.

Some Observations

Both spouses seemed to be well on their way toward balancing individual and couple needs. In this case, Tom's need to remain Roman Catholic was considered, along with his need to meet his wife's needs and his marriage's needs. Katina's personal need to remain actively involved with her faith and ethnic background have also been taken into account and a balance was met between her personal religious needs, Tom's needs, and the needs of their marriage.

Martha and Gus

Martha and Gus have been married for about eight years. Martha is a Mexican Catholic and Gus is Greek Orthodox. Gus is not very religious but is firmly connected to his Greek heritage. Martha has higher levels of religious commitment and equal amounts of connections to her ethnic background. As a result of their religious and cultural differences, this couple had argued about religion/culture issues and had been unsuccessful in deciding where they should go to church, and which ethnic traditions they should introduce into their family life.

Out of frustration, Gus decided that the couple should belong and pledge to the Greek Orthodox Church. However, Martha resisted this decision because she believed that she is "the religious one in the family" and she would eventually raise their children. A silent dispute developed around their religious and cultural choices that lingered and prevented them from meeting their personal, marital and future family needs.

Some Observations

In the second case, an imbalance existed between personal needs and couple needs. Gus' need to remain attached to his ethnic background caused him to disregard his wife and marriage's needs. Martha was equally at fault. Rather than seek a resolution, she was determined to imitate Gus' example and remained inflexible with regard to her personal religious and ethnic needs. This position caused her to place too much attention on her personal needs to the detriment of her spouse's and marriage's needs. Furthermore, this imbalance created some marital distress that will likely linger until it is addressed and some adjustments are made.

Principal Nuclear Family Needs

Honest, open conversation between spouses seemed key to religious well-being in inter-Christian family households. One participant stated, "We allowed our preferences about religion to go unattended for several years. This may have even postponed the birth of our first child. I would recommend that inter-Christian couples talk regularly, both before and after their marriage. Inter-Christian couples have to realize that conversation must take place regularly because marriages change and new things come up. Our failure to talk really made things hard on our marriage. We're better now. We have learned to talk more about the things that matter to us, and this has been really good for us and our family."

The issue of where their children would be baptized challenged inter-Christian couples. Couples stated that a failure to amicably resolve this issue could potentially jeopardize a family's religious development, as well as their children's religious development. For example, while considering the ongoing difficulties that she and her husband have had regarding their children's religious training, she stated, "For as long as I can remember we've disagreed over our children's religious development. Maybe that's why some of our children don't go to church any more."

Couples who determine to baptize their children in the Greek Orthodox Church stated that they struggled to help the non-Orthodox partner avoid "feeling like the odd person out" when it came to the family's religious life. One father stated, "One Sunday as we were driving home from church, my five-year-old innocently started talking about Daddy's church and the rest of the family's church. His comments made me feel really left out and somewhat separated from him and the rest of the family. I guess kids are pretty perceptive. When they see certain things around them, they say it like it is…. I have tried to be part of our children's religious development, but it's been tough when you can't receive the sacraments…. It's a hard reminder that some distance exists between me and the rest of the family in this area of our lives." In these instances, spouses admitted that the non-Orthodox parent should expect to feel somewhat out of place in this area of the family's life. They also stated that an acknowledgment of these feelings by either one or both spouses helped minimize the pain, and curtailed any destructive resentment that might build from these feelings. As one respondent stated, "When I get upset over the fact that our children belong to a different church than I do, my husband let's me ventilate, and that makes me feel a little better. But it doesn't last. Sooner or later, the hurt resurfaces…. Who knows, maybe one day I will decide to convert, but not now. The timing just isn't right yet."

Participants also maintained that homes that were conflicted over religion would likely produce children whose perception of religion would be negatively impacted. Negotiating clear, healthy boundaries that would respect each parent's sensitivities and preferences regarding their children's religious and spiritual development was repeatedly mentioned as important. Parents' disagreement about their children's religious training negatively impacted their children's religious development and created a source of family stress. While making this point, one respondent stated, "We realized the hard way that our constant bickering about the kids' religious upbringing didn't help them. One day, while we were arguing about something, our oldest daughter said, 'when I grow up I'm not going to church. It's not worth it.' And when she said that, I realized that we needed to stop the arguing and get together on this religious thing or our kids would either grow up without a religion or change to a different religion."

Along these same lines, these couples also felt that if their children were baptized and generally nurtured in one church tradition, this would enhance their efforts to religious and spiritual development. Making the choice – sometimes hard choice – to raise their children in one faith tradition was considered important to their children's religious development. "Consistency and structure is the name of the game, when it comes to children's development, and it's no different when it comes to children's religious formation. I really think that if we hadn't made the decision early on to raise them in one church; they would not have developed a religious bond. Today, they know that Daddy is Roman Catholic, and they respect their father's religious background. Nevertheless, they also know that they are Greek Orthodox. If we had decided to either raise them in both church traditions, or let them eventually choose, even though I can't prove it, I really believe they wouldn't be as religious as they are today."

Participants generally believed that children lack the ability to make sound decisions about their religious development. They repeatedly stated that parents must be a part of this decision well into their children's young adult lives. "Eventually our children will make a personal choice about religion," stated one respondent. "But when they're young, they can't do this themselves.... Left on their own, I suppose they would probably prefer to be outside with many of their friends on Sunday morning. So, its my opinion that the idea that children should be given the space to make choices about religion is silly. Children need their parents to help them make all sorts of important decisions, and religion is certainly no exception.

Learning how to draw healthy boundaries between themselves and their extended families in order to protect their families from unwanted intrusions was also repeatedly mentioned as being important. One respondent's observations made this point clear. "Early on in our marriage I felt like I was caught between what my wife wanted and what my parents wanted. On the one hand, my wife wanted us to worship in the Orthodox Church, and my parents wanted me to worship in the Catholic Church. Well, I can't tell you how uncomfortable that made me feel, because I felt stuck between these two strong pulls. Nevertheless, I got through it okay once I realigned my priorities and put my marriage first. After that I considered my parent's desires and needs, but never put them on an equal footing with my wife and family's needs." As couples learned how to love and honor their parents, while also drawing clear boundaries between themselves and their parents, this made things easier for everyone concerned.

Participants also repeatedly observed that when intermarried couples were unsuccessful in drawing clear boundaries between themselves and their extended families, some respondents were forced to subordinate and/or ignore their nuclear family needs in an effort to meet extended families' expectations and needs. One respondent stated, "We had to do the marriage thing in both churches to please both sides of our families." In another group, a participant stated, "We ended up baptizing some of our children in the Greek Orthodox Church, and some in the in-laws' church to make everyone happy. The only problem with that is it didn't make us and our children happy, and we regret that decision now."

Participants also indicated that they had a need to feel accepted as an intermarried family by the Greek Orthodox Church they attended. Quoting from a non-Orthodox participant, "I come to the Greek Orthodox Church because I feel as if it's an inter-Christian-friendly church, or a church that makes me and my husband feel accepted and comfortable. Father Lou is great about welcoming us, as are all the people in the church. We don't feel different or uncomfortable because we're an inter-Christian couple." When congregations were perceived as being accepting of intermarried couples, and open and friendly to newcomers and non-Greeks, couple and family participation was enhanced.

Sam and Fran's Failed Attempts at Balancing Individual, Couple and Family Needs

Sam and Fran have been married for twenty years. Sam was raised in a nominally Protestant household that did not place a great amount of importance on religious and ethnic matters. Fran was raised in a Greek Orthodox household that put a nominal value on religion, but a high value on ethnicity. As a result, when the couple had children they were baptized in the Greek Orthodox Church because of Fran's attachment to her ethnic background.

As time elapsed religion became more important to Sam, while Fran's level of religiosity remained constant. Moreover, Sam began insisting that the children attend his church because he felt that the Greek Orthodox Church his children attended undervalued religious training and overvalued ethnicity. Fran simply dismissed Sam's opinions and continued to bring the children to the Greek Orthodox Church because she wanted them to benefit from many of the same ethnic experiences that had positively contributed to her development. As such, the couple feuded for years over their children's religious development, and have only recently made amends.

Commenting about this in retrospect, Fran stated, "I know now that we were wrong. We should have listened more to each other. I can't help thinking that all our continued fighting over religious and ethnic issues was a big part of what soured our kids' attitudes toward organized religion because now that they are almost grown not one of them has any desire to belong to a church."

Sam also remarked, "I'm certain that what we did was not God's will. We got caught in a war of wills. It was my will against Fran's, and the kids got caught in the middle. If we had only stopped and thought about what was good for everyone, I believe God would have helped us make some compromises that would have met everyone's needs."

Some Additional Observations

In this case, both Fran and Sam focused their attention on each spouse's individual needs, but failed to consider marital and family needs. As such, this imbalance negatively impacted individual, couple and family satisfaction. Their lingering feuding also adversely affected their children's religious development.

Principal Extended Family Needs

Extended family members, especially parents, have a need to know that their adult children will remain connected to them in some form after they leave home. When adult children honor family traditions, parents are somewhat reassured that their adult children have retained some connection with them. Adult children who intermarry may sometimes cause their parents to wonder if they will lose touch with their adult intermarried children. "I couldn't understand what the big fuss was," stated one respondent. "The person I chose to marry was intelligent, came from a good family, and had all the qualities that they had wanted me to look for. So, when I started dating my wife, and I started getting all this grief, I really struggled to understand what the problem was. Then one day, it occurred to me. They were worried that they might lose complete touch with me. So when I assured them that they wouldn't, things started getting considerably better between us. I guess they needed to know that I wasn't abandoning the family and they weren't losing me."

Grandparents also have a need for their grandchildren to experience their religious and cultural background. One reason for this may be connected to the grandparents' desire to see that their grandchildren's religious, moral and spiritual needs will be met. "I know that my parents worried over my decision to baptize our children in the Greek Orthodox Church. Until they were convinced that they would be getting a good Christian grounding, they were really concerned. After they found out that the Greek Church is a Christian Church, they felt better – not perfect, but better," related one non-Orthodox participant.

Grandparents also want to cultivate connections between themselves and their grandchildren. One way of ensuring this is through the religious and cultural traditions they hold in common with their grandchildren. When intermarried couples determine to baptize and raise their children in a religious tradition other than their own, this can be perceived as threatening to these connections. "Informing my parents that our son would be baptized Greek Orthodox really upset them. And I couldn't understand why until I realized that they were concerned about how this would compromise their relationship with our kids."

Balancing Individual, Couple and Extended Family Needs

Couples are embedded within at least two extended family subsystems. Moreover, both sides of the family will have needs similar to those mentioned above. In an effort to meet these needs, extended family members may apply overt or covert pressure on intermarried couples and families. As such, balancing individual, couple and extended family needs is a talent that intermarried couples must master. The following two examples make this clear. In the first example, extended family needs and pressures threatened to negatively impact an inter-married couple's marriage. In the second example, extended family needs threatened intermarried family stability.

John and Mary

John, age 27, and Mary, age 25, have been married for about one year. John is a first generation Greek Orthodox, and Mary is a non-practicing Roman Catholic from a mixed ethnic back-ground. This couple is happily married, but that was not al-ways the case during their first year of marriage. Some of the reasons why are chronicled below.

When John and Mary began dating, John's parents were quick to point out that "It was fine that he date a non-Greek for fun-and-games' sake, but he should only permit himself to become serious with a Greek girl, since marriages with non-Greeks do not work out." John politely listened to his parents, but because of his increasing affection for Mary, he could not agree with them, and continued to date Mary. John also decided to hide his parent's dissatisfaction from Mary, fearing that if he shared this information, it would somehow compromise their relationship.

Several months passed, John and Mary became very seri-ous, and one day John proposed marriage and Mary accepted. The next day, because he was unable to predict how his par-ents might react, and not wanting his fiancée to hear any nega-tive remarks about their decision to wed, John privately shared this news with his parents.

When John's parents received this news, they began to issue ultimatums like the following one: "If you marry this girl we will disown you." But as the argument continued, and they saw that they were getting nowhere with John, their tone changed. They began to state that they would tolerate this de-cision for his sake, but would also "not be surprised if their marriage did not survive."

Since John knew that Mary was a non-practicing Catholic, he asked her if she would agree to get married in the Greek Orthodox Church, stating, this would please his parents.

Wishing to improve her rather distant and cold relationship with John's parents, Mary consented to this suggestion, and the couple married in the Greek Orthodox Church. Unfortunately, however, Mary's good will gesture did nothing to improve her relationship with her in-laws, and they continued to interact in a distant but cordial manner.

About six months after the marriage, John's parents approached him, strongly urging him to ask Mary to join the Greek Orthodox Church. They also told him that he "should convince Mary to convert, since this would be good for their children and family." As a result of these and other similar remarks, John went home that night and proposed the following suggestion to his wife. "I think we should have a family church, and since we were married in the Greek Church, we should join my family's church. I also think that it's time that you think about converting, because it would be good for our future children."

Dumbfounded by these remarks, Mary responded, "Where in the world has this come from, John? You've never suggested to me that religion was important to you before this day. I don't know, there's a lot to think about here."

Not wishing to disclose who prompted him to make this statement, John defensively responded, "So what's wrong with having a family church and being the same religion? And what's to think about? It's no big deal. We go once in a while and everyone's happy."

Upon hearing this last statement, Mary then stated, "It's your parents who put you up to this, isn't it? They have fed you these ideas, and now you're siding with them, aren't you?

"And what if it was?" stated John, even more defensively.

"Do you know how that makes me feel when you talk to them about things that concern us, before you talk to me? It makes me feel betrayed, John. And another thing, how can I trust you if I think you're withholding information from me?"

That night was a long and emotional evening for both John and Mary. John finally told Mary the truth about his parent's feeling for them. He asked for Mary's forgiveness, and promised never to withhold information from her again. The couple then formulated some new boundaries that would not allow John's parents to divide the couple again.

Some Observations
   In this example, John placed an inordinate focus on his need to satisfy his parents, as well as their needs. In the process, he lost focus of his marriage's needs. In addition, Mary seems to have placed an unequal amount of attention on John and his parent's needs, but ignored her needs. Finally, the parents sought to meet their needs and John's needs, but ignored Mary's needs. Fortunately, this couple understood the source of the problem and entered into some productive discussion that led to the establishment of some healthy boundaries and a greater balance between individual, couple and extended family needs.

Balancing Individual, Couple, Children's and Extended Family Needs
   Just as couples must seek to protect their marriage from unwanted extended family intrusions, they must also seek to draw healthy boundaries between themselves and their extended families when it comes to how they will raise their children. Just as individual spouses desire that their children be exposed to certain religious and cultural traditions that serve to enhance their personal development, grandparents tend to have similar needs. Moreover, in an effort to realize these needs, grandparents sometimes seek to apply overt or covert pressure on intermarried spouses and/or couples.
   Intermarried spouses will often be challenged to meet individual needs, marital needs, their children's needs, and extended family needs. To the extent that they reach a balance between all these subsystems needs, stability and satisfaction will exist at all levels. To the extent that balance is not achieved, this failure will have a negative effect on one or both spouses, their marriage, the nuclear family, their children's development, and nuclear family and extended family interactions and transactions. The following illustration makes this point.

Bob and Sophia

Bob's Catholic parents were delighted to hear that Sophia, who was Greek Orthodox, was expecting. Bob's mother, a devout Catholic, began pressuring Bob and Sophia to make a decision about baptism. To complicate matters further, Sophia was the more religious partner and would likely be responsible for their future child's religious training.

Bob and Sophia both felt caught between Bob's mother's overt demands to have their child baptized in the Catholic Church, and the knowledge that Sophia would do a much better job at ensuring that their future children would develop a healthy religious conscience. After several conversations, the couple decided that they needed to tell Bob's mother that they appreciated her concern, but that they (as parents) would make the final decision about baptism. While this created some initial tension between Bob's mother and the couple, eventually the tension dissipated as the couple continued to hold fast to their decision. Reflecting back on their decision, Bob stated, "I know it was hard on my Mom, but it was hard on all of us. Ultimately we couldn't meet everyone's needs. I love my Mom, and I think she knows this, but for our children's religious welfare we decided on the Orthodox Church because it was the best thing for the children and our family."

Some Observations

Fortunately, this couple determined to make decisions that were good for their children and family and they did not succumb to Bob's mother's pressure. However, if they had, such a decision could have potentially created an imbalance and some trouble between Bob and Mary, and between Mary and her mother-in-law. Such a decision could likely have had lasting negative effects on the children's religious and spiritual development.

Faith Community Needs

Faith community needs can create additional problems for intermarried spouses. This is so because faith communities seek to indoctrinate their adherents into a specific belief system while also seeking to communicate the correctness of what they believe to their adherents. To that end, intermarried couples will experience some very real challenges in their efforts to remain faithful to their respective faith traditions while seeking to balance their individual needs, marital needs, family needs, and in some instances, their extended family needs. Consider the following example.

Jean and George

Jean was raised a Missouri Synod Lutheran while George was raised in the Greek Orthodox Church. Both were highly religious and tried to live by their respective church's rules. Fortunately, this couple spent lengthy amounts of time working out the differences that existed between their two faith traditions. They concluded that the only way they could get married would be if they respected each other's religious differences. They also concluded that they would agree to disagree over issues regarding their faith traditions, and would not allow their religious differences to become divisive and undermine marital stability. Although this approach seemed to generally work, their were times when both partners broke this rule, and engaged in debate over religious matters. These instances were few in number, however, and over time decreased in frequency, since both spouses came to believe that this was unholy behavior that was "Satan's doing and not anchored in God's will."

Some Observations

Many intermarried couples experience negative residual effects from the theological differences that exist between their two faith communities. Moreover, in some instances many of their inter-Christian differences serve to create marital distance and strife. Couples who are not careful to respect their partner's religious differences and enter into theological debates over religion can undermine individual, couple and family stability.

Couples who determine to allow their religious leaders to work out theological differences, and who seek to emphasize what they hold in common, tend to be able to strike a balance between individual, couple and family needs.

When Dominant American Cultural Values Conflict with Spouses' Subcultural Needs

Our dominant American culture also has certain needs and priorities that ensure its survival. Chief among our American culture's needs is our society's efforts to respect the needs of its very diverse, multicultural citizens. To achieve this end, concepts such as tolerance and respect for difference have gained privilege and favor in our society.

Intermarried couples are generally in agreement with concepts that teach tolerance, respect, and acceptance for diversity. Yet, they can sometimes experience some distress when dominant cultural values clash with their religious and ethnic traditions, beliefs, and rules.

This can create some challenges for these types of couples, since their immediate inclination is to embrace concepts that encourage inclusiveness. Being respectful to certain exclusive religious and ethnic traditions, as well as being committed to the broader culture's commitment for promoting acceptance for cultural diversity, can and does create challenges at the individual, marital, family, extended family, and faith community levels. Finding a balance between all these different subsystems' needs can present some formidable challenges. Sally and Plato's story illustrates this point. In this example, the couple describes a clash between subculture needs and the dominant American culture's needs.

Sally and Plato

Sally and Plato regularly attended the Greek Orthodox Church. Both were rather offended, however, when the priest would regularly extol the merits of ancient Greek culture, but did not mention any other ethnic groups' contributions. As a result, both felt as if their priest was engaging in a subtle form of nationalism and ethnocentrism which was offensive to them. They decided to speak to the priest in order to communicate this concern.

The priest listened respectfully, then stated that it was not his intention to disparage other ethnic groups, and that his main objective was simply to celebrate and applaud the accomplishments of his congregation's ethnic roots. The couple then pointed out that there were many non-Greeks attending their church and wondered how this was affecting those, like Sally, who were non-Greeks. They also stated that they did not find the church's efforts to celebrate ethnicity offensive as long as the church did not purposely engage in ethnocentric behavior.

Their parish priest could not agree with this latter observation and stated, "I find what I am doing to be totally American." In response, the couple pointed out that people should not have to feel this type of discomfort when they come to church, and they wondered if this was not counterproductive to the church's efforts to meet the needs of its non-Greek members. In the end, the priest listened and stated, "You've made some valid points that I must consider more carefully. I want to extol the merits of Hellenism, but not at the expense of alienating our non-Greek members. I will try to explore ways of doing both in a more respectful manner."

Some Observations

Striking a balance between dominant cultural values and subcultural values can create some challenges. On the one hand, many intermarried couples generally feel some discomfort when a skewed emphasis is placed on extolling one given cultural background – for our discussion, Hellenism. On the other hand, the Greek Orthodox Archdiocese's founders were decidedly from a Hellenistic background, and most of its members have blood ties to Greece. As such, a conflict of interest can sometimes create tension. Intermarried couples feel more comfortable with inclusive language that celebrates ethnicity. Many clergy and faithful have a need to extol Hellenistic culture, but do not do this at the expense of other's feelings and needs. Some respectful discussion with regard to these conflicting needs is, thus, necessary at all levels of the Archdiocese. This discussion should seek to strike a balance between all segments of the Greek Orthodox Archdiocese's needs.

Chapter Nine

MARITAL AND FAMILY LIFE CYCLE CHALLENGES

Pray together at home and go to church… Remind one another that nothing in life is to be feared, except offending God. If your marriage is like this, your perfection will rival the holiest of monks. – *St. John Chrysostom*

It is generally understood that as we mature, we encounter different challenges across the life cycle. For example, while teens are busy trying to form their own opinions about life, young adults might be trying to acquire financial independence, middle aged adults might be busy raising families and cultivating careers, and older adults may be preoccupied in reviewing their lives and finding positive closure. Just as the individual encounters different challenges as he or she matures and ages, families also experience different challenges as family members mature. This chapter will present some of the challenges that inter-Christian, intercultural spouses, couples, and families might encounter as they pass through the family life cycle. These challenges will be presented in story form through a series of interviews followed by additional information. The interviews do not involve real couples. The couples you will meet in the following pages are composites of typical couples that participated in the IRP and attend our churches. Intermarried couples that familiarize themselves with the challenges listed below will be in a better position to embrace these challenges and use them as opportunities for growth.

Challenges of Inter-Christian, Intercultural Dating

Let me introduce you to Denise, age 24, whose religious and ethnic roots are Polish Catholic, and to Gus, age 26, a Greek Orthodox Christian. They have been married for 2 years. They live in the southwest where Denise works as a bank clerk and Gus is a sales representative. Both describe their relationship as stable and happy, but also admit to having worked through a number of challenges over the past several years "especially when we were dating."

When asked to elaborate, Denise smiled, and then thoughtfully responded. "Sometimes it was like a bad dream that never seemed to want to end."

They both smiled, then she continued. "From the beginning, our parents discouraged us from dating each other. Gus' parents wanted him to date more Greek girls, and my mother (my parents are divorced) wasn't too keen with the idea that I was dating someone from the Greek Orthodox Faith."

At this point, Gus entered into the conversation, "More Greek girls – that's a hoot. My Church is small, and there were only a limited number of Greek girls that I could date. And yes, I attended some YAL[1] conferences in hopes of connecting with someone, but I just never felt the same kind of chemistry between the girls I met at those conferences and what existed between me and Denise."

Denise smiled at the last comment and then continued. "We met at Kansas State in my junior and his senior year. At first we wanted to keep everything relaxed and casual, but soon we realized that this wasn't like any other relationship either of us had experienced."

Gus picked up the conversation and agreed, "I think we both pretty much knew after a few months that this was something special. By the end of our first year of dating, things had gotten pretty serious, and we began to discuss marriage."

"And just when everything was going so well, we decided to inform our parents of some of our feelings and intentions.

That's when things got interesting," offered Denise. "At first, our parents were politely unresponsive to the news. But as we continued seeing each other, the disappointment and concerns from both sides started coming with regular frequency. There was this awful tension between my mother and Gus, and Gus' parents grew rather cold and aloof toward me."

"My parents kept on trying to dismiss my feelings for Denise, as if they were some fanciful whim. When this didn't work, they began to apply pressure on me to break things off," Gus stated while shaking his head. "My parents also asked me not to bring Denise to the house or to church. And they kept suggesting Greek girls' names that I hadn't even dated. It was really insane."

"Then there was the issue of the Church wedding," recalled Denise. "The Orthodox Church wouldn't recognize the Catholic Sacrament of Marriage. To accommodate this rule, we began talking about getting married in the Orthodox Church. I think this made it easier for Gus' parents, and broke some ice between us all, but at the same time irritated and hurt my Mom. She believed that the wedding should take place in the bride's church. To make things worse, Gus couldn't explain his Church's position. It was a real mess again, and people weren't talking to each other. Things didn't look good."

Gus continued, "I think one of the major turning points was when we decided that if that's the way our parents were going to act, then we would simply get married by a Justice of the Peace. In addition, we proceeded to respectfully inform them of this decision. I really think that's when both sides began softening their position and accepted the marriage, but also subtly predicted its demise."

"I also think that our priests' advice really helped," stated Denise. "After asking us some rather pointed questions, both priests were super supportive and guided us through these and other land mines, until things began to become tolerable."

"Things are better now," Gus added with some relief in his voice. "My folks really love Denise, and Denise's mother has warmed up to me. But for a while, things were really touch and go, and I wasn't certain how our desire to marry would affect our relationship with our parents."

Challenges Dating Couples Might Face
Most inter-Christian and intercultural couples can expect to encounter challenges from their family during the dating process that are connected to their religious and cultural differences.

- While some tension can, and often does, develop during the dating process, it is important to note that much of this tension is healthy. It compels couples to face some of the realities behind their decision to enter into an inter-Christian and intercultural marriage.

- Parents may politely tolerate their adult children's dating partners until the dating process moves from a casual to a more serious level. Parents may then seek to undermine the dating process when couples become serious by revealing displeasure and withholding their blessings. In most instances, this occurs because parents care for their children and are concerned for their well-being.

- It is also important to mention that while some tension typically emerges between the dating couple and their extended families, this tension generally does not result in cutoffs between adult children and parents. A reduction in intensity and regularity of this tension usually occurs over time as new and healthy boundaries develop that meet (a) the individual dating partners' needs, (b) the couple's needs, (c) the extended family's needs, and (d) the faith community's needs and expectations.

- Conflicting faith community rules can also create challenges. Dating partners may feel caught between desires to have a church wedding, meet their own individual and couple needs, and please both sides of the family. They also need to respect and comply with their respective church's rules.

Couple Challenges After Marriage
   During the first few years of marriage, couples seek to blend two separate lives into one. Along with the typical challenges that most single-church couples encounter, intermarried couples must negotiate a host of challenges related to their religious, cultural and perhaps, racial differences. This section will illustrate some of those challenges.

Meet Tina and Harold
   Tina, age 25, and Harold, age 25, have been married for almost two years. Tina is a second generation Greek-American Orthodox Christian. Harold was raised in the Methodist Church and comes from a Scottish-Irish background. Both met at a small liberal arts college, dated for about one year, and were subsequently engaged and married in the Greek Orthodox Church.

   When asked to describe some of their experiences since marriage, Harold began, "It's been an interesting two years. For a while, I wondered what I had gotten myself into, because we were having lots of difficulty adjusting to each other's backgrounds. But I suppose our love for each other buffered us from any serious negative residual effects."

   Nodding in agreement, Tina remarked, "It's been harder than I first supposed it might be for me also, but I think it was harder for Harold. He seems to be the one who had to make most of the adjustments."

   Asked to elaborate, Harold continued. "I wasn't exactly embraced with open arms, by Tina's family before the marriage. Tina's Mom even went so far as to tell me that it was difficult for her when she realized that Tina would be marrying a non-Greek. And to make things worse, for a long time after the wedding, most of her family seemed cold and distant toward me."

   Tina interjected, "I don't think it was that long, Honey – maybe a few months. When they realized that I was happy, and that you weren't going away, they began to soften."

"I suppose," said Harold. "But to me, it seemed like a long time. And then when everyone began warming up to me, this was also an awkward time. Members of my family tend to relate differently to one another. From what I've discovered, Greek families tend to be more involved with each other. They also tend to be more emotionally expressive people. So, when Tina's family started treating me like one of the family, it was rather difficult for me to handle because I didn't really know how to interpret all this new and unfamiliar behavior. But don't misunderstand me. I like Tina's family, and have learned to adjust to their way of interacting with each other. It was just difficult at first, that's all."

Harold paused, looked at Tina as if to ask if she has anything to add, then continued. "Then there were the differences in our religious traditions. I was raised in the Methodist Church and wasn't really going to church very much when I met Tina. Since she has such a strong faith in God, to please her, I began attending the Greek Orthodox Church with her after we got married. Nevertheless, it was really frustrating for me, because I couldn't understand the rituals, and a lot of the services were conducted in Greek. And worse than this, whenever I asked Tina to explain something, she wasn't really able to offer me a complete explanation."

"That's true," Tina said. "I love my church. It's the only church I've found that makes me feel comfortable. I went to Harold's church a few times, but things were too unfamiliar. Anyhow, as I was saying, when Harold started asking me questions about the Orthodox Church, I realized how much I didn't know. So we started picking up books, and even going to some of Fr. Peter's Wednesday night adult education classes, which proved to be an enriching experience for us both."

Harold looked at Tina with a smile and declared, "I think that maybe it's been more of an enriching experience for you than for me. But I will say one thing, when Tina fasts, or displays icons in our home, or when I'm at my in-laws and they crack Easter eggs or cut the New Years bread – at least I'm not lost."

This part of our conversation appeared to be ending. Both spouses were quiet, until Tina made the following additional observation. "Even though we've spent most of our time describing the difficulties that Harold experienced trying to adjust to my background, I think that he would agree that we've worked hard at trying to combine the best of both of our backgrounds."

Nodding in agreement, Harold stated, "I think that's a fair statement. I also think we're far more like other couples than we are different. And the few differences we've spoken about seem to have enriched our lives. I also think that our future children will benefit from our different backgrounds."

Challenges After Marriage

- Couples like Tina and Harold who participated in IRP, repeatedly stated that they were faced with challenges during the first few years of marriage. The results also suggest that couples that viewed their different religious and cultural backgrounds as enriching were less inclined to experience long term negative residual effects. Conversely, couples who continued to experience difficulties related to their religious and cultural differences, tended to perceive them as drawbacks, and were more likely to experience lingering marital and family conflict.

- While both partners may experience some degree of culture shock in their efforts to adapt to their partner's religious and cultural background, results from the IRP suggest that the non-Orthodox partner may be apt to experience more discomfort when introduced to their partner's Greek Orthodox background. In most cases, the insecurity and unfamiliarity with their partner's cultural and religious idiosyncrasies tended to resolve with time.

- Spouses also described an awkward period between themselves and their in-laws. In most instances, this period did not last long. However, in some instances, their relationship with

their in-laws remained distant and cold. The non-Greek Orthodox partners seemed more likely to experience more of these
types of challenges than their Greek Orthodox partners did.

- While it may not be apparent from this interview, results
from the IRP indicate that it was important for newly married
couples to draw healthy boundaries between themselves and
their parents. Keeping out unwanted extended family intrusions was important to couples' efforts to mold and shape a life
together.

- Finally, most of these couples indicated that their faith in
God was indispensable in their efforts to strike a balance between personal, couple, and extended family needs. Given their
religious differences, some couples were challenged to find
ways to pray together. Those who struggled to develop a prayer
life together found that in doing so, stresses and strains of developing a life together were minimized.

When the Children Arrive

Most couples decide to begin a family after a few years of
marriage. Along with the typical challenges that single-church,
single cultural couples face, intermarried couples can expect to
encounter additional challenges related to their religious and
cultural differences. The challenges described in the following
interview are typical of what intermarried couples face when
they consider starting a family.

Meet Bill and Maria

Bill, age 28, and Maria, age 29, have been married four years.
Bill is a civil engineer and Maria is an elementary school teacher.
Bill was cradle Episcopalian, attended services sporadically
since the couple's first child arrived, but retained membership
in the Episcopalian Church. Maria is a second generation Greek-
American and an active member of her local church. The couple
has two children, Nicole (2), and Jason (3 months). Both spouses
described their marriage as being stable and happy, but also

candidly indicate that they have faced numerous "difficulties over the past two years" related to their religious and cultural differences.

Asked to describe some of these challenges, Maria began, "When I look back at the past four years of marriage, there are a number of really good memories, but there have also been a number of difficulties. Perhaps one of the most upsetting things for me has been our inability to come to terms with our religious and cultural differences. We're both strong willed people, and I guess that hasn't helped."

Bill agreed and continued the conversation. "I don't know. It didn't really concern me when Maria wanted to get married in the Greek Orthodox Church. I sort of understood that it was important to her and her family. Some of our major problems began when we started thinking about having children."

"That's pretty accurate," remarked Maria. "Before the children, we sort of alternated, attending both churches. In addition, I'll admit that, the services in Bill's church didn't always do that much for me, I went because I knew it pleased Bill and my in-laws. Nevertheless, when we started thinking about having children that's when things began to get more complicated. After Nicole was born – our first-born – I assumed we were going to baptize her in the Greek Church, and that's when things got bad between us. It turned out that Bill wanted to talk about this decision more, and I considered the decision made, and I didn't want to talk about it. Looking back now, I think Bill thought I was being very stubborn, and this made him angrier and angrier. Nevertheless, the real truth is that I was afraid that if we talked about this, our kids would be baptized in his church or another church. And that really upset me."

At this point, Bill added to his wife's comments. "Yeah, we really had some very heated arguments… and it's not that I was necessarily against baptizing the kids in the Greek Orthodox Church, because our churches are really similar. My main complaint was that she arrived at this decision with her folks, and kept me out of the loop." He paused for a moment, and then continued. "I guess down deep inside, I always knew that our kids would attend the Greek Orthodox Church, because Maria's with the children more, and she's always taken the lead when it comes to any decisions connected to religion. But when I found out that she and her folks had made the decision without consulting me, that really got to me, and I resisted the whole idea."

"It got so bad at one point," Maria continued, "that I left the house one night after a particularly heated argument and went to my parent's home. Thankfully, my father encouraged me to return home and work things out with Bill. So, I went back home, and that night we had our first real discussion about this issue. I'm happy to state that our decision – not my decision or Bill's decision – was to baptize Nicole and our other future children in the Greek Orthodox Church."

"That was kind of hard for me," stated Bill. "As the children have grown, we've all but stopped attending the Episcopalian Church, almost exclusively attending the Greek Orthodox Church because we want what's best for their religious upbringing." Bill paused for a moment. "It's also been kind of hard because I'm feeling more and more like the 'odd-man-out' when it comes to our family's religious life. The fact that I can't really participate in an active way at church with my family and often feel more like 'the visitor' kind of hurts. Moreover, I have thought about converting, I'm just not ready to leave my religious tradition behind. Who knows, maybe I'll never be ready. For now I've chosen to attend the Greek Church mostly for my family and kids."

Maria offered the last comment on this subject by stating, "Every time I think about the sacrifice that Bill made for me and the kids, I'm really grateful to him. I don't think I could have made the same sacrifice."

Challenges Related to Starting a Family
   - If couples fail to discuss where their children will be baptized, and in which church they will be raised before marriage,

some conversation regarding these questions will likely occur around the time of the first child's arrival. Couples with equally strong attachments to their religious and ethnic backgrounds may have more difficulties negotiating these questions, than couples where one partner is more religious than the other. Couples with equally low levels of religious and ethnic attachments may not experience much conflict resolving these questions.

- Finding ways to strike a balance between each spouse's desire to baptize the future children in his/her faith community, to do what is best for them, and their desire to respectfully consider their spouse's opinion, can create tension between couples. Unspoken assumptions before marriage regarding this issue can often trigger disappointment and hurt feelings that lead to marital conflict. Such feelings and thoughts can potentially linger for years and undermine the family members' religious and spiritual development.

- The grandparents' yearnings to see their children baptized and raised in their faith community can also present some challenges to intermarried couples. Grandparents may apply pressure on their adult children that can create even more tension between couples who have conflicted feelings over the issue of baptism. Couples will be challenged to find respectful ways of drawing healthy boundaries between themselves and their extended families in their efforts to arrive at a mutually satisfying decision regarding their children's baptism. Unwanted grandparent intrusions and pressures can serve to convolute parents' efforts to resolve this issue as well as compromise growing relationships with extended family members.

- While the above conversation does not infer this, some couples will also struggle with the Greek tradition that calls for Greek parents to name the first born son after the Greek Orthodox spouse's father. The Greek Orthodox partner may feel a deep need to honor the parent in this way while the non-Orthodox partner frequently views this tradition as a cultural intrusion. Finding ways of striking a balance between personal, couple, and extended family needs in this situation can generate marital, family and extended family tension. In some instances, couples will determine to give their children two names, a legal name and a baptismal name. In other cases, one or the other partner will make a concession. In the worst of cases, one partner or the other partner will unilaterally make a decision regarding this issue that can potentially create lingering resentment in the other spouse.

- If the couple decides to baptize their children in the Greek Orthodox Church, the non-Orthodox partner and his or her extended family may feel somewhat short changed especially since Orthodox pastoral guidelines prohibit non-Orthodox participation in the Sacraments. The Orthodox partner may feel varying degrees of resentment for these rules from the non-Orthodox spouse and his or her extended family. Finding ways of not personalizing this resentment will be helpful to nuclear and extended family stability and well-being.

- In order to meet the children's growing religious and spiritual needs, couples usually choose to attend the church where their children were baptized. When intermarried couples determine to baptize their child in the Greek Orthodox Church, and subsequently decide to attend the Orthodox Church, the non-Orthodox partner may struggle to avoid feeling like the odd-man-out when the family attends Divine Liturgy together. This is the case because non-Orthodox cannot participate in the Sacramental life of the Orthodox Church. Being aware of this potential pitfall can help both partners work through negative feelings and thoughts that might undermine family members' religious and spiritual development.

- Lingering hurt feelings related to the children's cultural development can be unhealthy for a couple's marriage and their children's development. Finding ways to address hurt feelings can be challenging since such discussions are viewed as potentially uncomfortable and counterproductive. Failure to ease hurt feelings could be detrimental to marital and family religious well-being.

When the Children Begin Maturing
John, age 35, and Toni, age 34, have been married for ten years. John is a fourth generation Greek Orthodox Christian and Toni comes from an Italian Roman Catholic background. They are both professionals and admit to certain "lingering marital and family disagreements" associated with their different religious backgrounds. They have three children, John (8), Sophia (6), and Thomas (4).

Toni began. "When it comes to our children's religious training, I don't know, it's been kind of frustrating for me over the years." She paused for a moment, visibly upset, and continued. "To please John and his parents, I relented to baptizing the children in the Greek Church. But I'm often very sorry that I gave in and agreed to this."

John interrupted his wife. "That's not entirely true, Honey. It had very little to do with me. Well, what I mean, is that I didn't care nearly as much as my parents about where the kids would be baptized. They're the ones that applied the pressure. So to keep the peace in the family, I remember asking you if you wouldn't mind if we baptized them in the Greek Church."

"Well that's not exactly how I remember things. But anyway, be that as if may, I agreed, and we decided to baptize them Greek Orthodox." She paused again to collect herself, and then proceeded. "And maybe I wouldn't feel so upset and resentful if John took an interest in their religious training, but he hasn't. Don't get me wrong, he's a good man and a great father, but he's not really a very religious person. He doesn't really know his religion, and he hardly ever goes to church. So, the responsibility to bring them up in the Greek Church has fallen on my shoulders. But I don't know the Greek Church like I know my church, so the end result is that they have grown up without much religious training."

"I know that Toni is right," John stated with some regret. "But I've got work commitments that keep me busy all week, and when Sundays roll around, I need to unwind. To be honest, Church has never done much for me. I simply don't understand it. I respect it and value religion, but I don't get anything out of it. So, I guess I've chosen other ways of using my time to unwind on Sundays."

"We've had this conversation over and over again," Toni stated with some frustration and then addressed John. "The remedy might have been for us to have chosen to attend the Catholic Church. However, I rather doubt that also, because I think kids religious training requires the involvement of both parents." Toni paused for a moment, then continued in a slightly different direction. "I'm not Greek Orthodox, so I don't really know the services, and can't participate in communion. It was okay when the children were younger, but now that they're growing older, they ask me questions that I don't know how to answer. So because John isn't interested in going to Church, we don't go very often – maybe we might go on Christmas and Easter."

John remained quiet, so Toni continued. "And do you know what really hurts these days? As the kids matured, I would have liked for them to experience their first communion and confirmation in the Catholic Church as I did. Those were really special times for me, and I regret the fact that they will not have these experiences."

At this juncture, John appeared very serious and genuinely moved by what his wife has stated, and then offered the following comments. "I didn't know you felt this strongly about this. I guess it's because religion has been such an insignificant factor in our lives. Maybe we need to discuss this more when we get home. Maybe, it's time for me to make some changes. Maybe, I've been really selfish."

"Yes, maybe you have John. Maybe we both have. I hope we can resolve this before they get much older, and it's too late. I hope it's not too late now... I guess I'm really glad we had this conversation. "

Challenges Related to Maturing Children's Religious Needs

- As children mature, a couple's focus will shift from a pre-occupation with their own relationship to a greater focus on their children's needs. As a result, many couples that have previously only been nominally interested in religion may show an increased interest in religious matters. While most intermarried couples that attend the Greek Orthodox Church may not be nearly as conflicted as John and Toni over their religious differences, many will encounter challenges such as those presented here.

- The intermarried couple's religious differences can potentially impede their children's efforts to develop a religious identity. In the couple's zeal to be respectful to both partners' religious backgrounds, they can potentially forget that children need time to bond to a faith group and develop a religious identity. When parents fail to provide their children with a consistent faith experience in one church, this can prevent them from developing a strong religious identity. Striking a balance between helping their children develop a keen respect for both parents' religious traditions, while also helping them bond to one faith tradition, can be a tricky proposition that intermarried parents may likely encounter.

- As children mature, they ask questions in an effort to piece their world together. As they observe their parent's different religious habits, they will naturally ask questions. Sometimes these questions can present real challenges to the parents. Typical questions may be: "Why doesn't Mom receive communion with us?" or, "Why doesn't Dad come to church with us?" or, "Why does Dad do his cross differently?" When parents are presented with these questions, they are not familiar enough with their own faith tradition and/or their partner's faith tradition to offer an adequate answer.

- The parent who has agreed to baptize the children in the partner's faith tradition can also end up feeling some distance between himself/herself and the children in this area of their developing lives. This is especially the case when the parent has a moderate to strong religious attachment. The parent might also feel some degree of loss as a result of their decision to baptize the children in the partner's church.

- Spouses who have had their children baptized in their church can also end up feeling some guilt when they become aware their partner's feelings. In these instances, ongoing discussion is necessary to ensure that these negative feelings do not impact couple and family religious and spiritual well-being.

- Extended family pressures are generally of minimal concern at this point in the family life cycle. Couples have generally managed to develop healthy boundaries between themselves and their respective families. Nevertheless, like John and Toni, couples might experience challenges related to previous decisions made as a result of extended family pressure. In these cases, it is important to identify the source of the problem and seek to remedy it without placing blame. In addition, while boundaries between extended families and nuclear families have been drawn, couples need to be aware that extended family members might attempt to challenge these boundaries. They should remember that even though grandparents may be well-meaning, they need to stand together at these times, and respectfully remind extended family that they, as parents, will make decisions about their children's religious development and well-being.

- Finally, couples should remember that when inter-Christian families experience these challenges, most report working through them and emerging unscathed. Prayer and Christian understanding go a long way toward helping couples reach a healthy resolution.

When Children Reach Adolescence

Basil, age 43, and Jane, age 38, have been married for eighteen years. Basil is Greek Orthodox and a master sergeant in the military. Jane is Southern Baptist and manages a local restaurant. The couple has two teenagers, Maria (15) and John (13). Both children have been baptized in the Greek Orthodox Church. They reside in a small southwestern city and periodically attend a Greek Orthodox mission parish some fifty miles from their home.

They also admit to having had mixed experiences while seeking an Orthodox Church, due to military reassignments. For the past several years, they have contemplated leaving the Orthodox Church, but have yet to arrive at a decision to do so. Our conversation began from this point.

"I suppose I can't pin the fault entirely on the Greek Orthodox Church," stated Basil. "But I'm beginning to believe my long-time insistence that we attend the Greek Orthodox Church has made it harder for my family to have much of a religious life. Don't get me wrong, I'm sure part of the problem rests in the fact that we're a military family, and we've moved around a lot."

"That's not true," Jane crisply replied. "I'll admit that moving has frequently made it difficult for us to make many lasting church family connections, but our regular moves aren't really that much a part of the problem. The real problem is that Basil has always wanted some connection with his Greek heritage, but wasn't really very religious until recently."

"There's some truth to what Jane is saying here. Up until recently, I haven't been the most religious person, and what seemed important to me was having some contact with my Greek heritage. But today - for reasons I won't explain here - I feel differently. I'm still very proud of my nationality, but I'm equally interested these days in finding a church home that meets my family's needs," Basil stated.

Basil paused for a moment to determine if his wife had anything to add. Noting her silence, he continued. "Today I am wondering how the Greek Orthodox Church fits into my family's religious needs, especially our kids' needs. What I mean is that my wife is not Greek, and my children really don't identify with the ethnic side of the Greek Church. So lately, I've been wondering if we need to try another church."

"I gave in to Basil when we got married, and agreed to attend the Greek Church," Jane remarked, breaking into the conversation abruptly. "But I guess I've never fully accepted this decision, and we've had one battle after the next ever since. I've always wanted to attend a more Bible centered church, and as the children grew older, I believed that a Church with a Bible centered perspective, rather than an ethnic centered perspective, was better suited for them."

At this juncture in our conversation, Jane paused, and looked at her husband as if she is asking him to help her explain her next point. Basil accommodated her silent request by stating, "I suppose what my wife might want to say at this point is that she's never really felt accepted in the Greek Orthodox Church."

"That's part of it," Jane stated, and then pauses momentarily to collect herself. She appeared visibly upset. "Sometimes I've felt like a second class citizen because I'm not Greek Orthodox... but that's not my real struggle these days. I'm especially concerned with our children's spiritual welfare. Over the past few years, Maria, our oldest, says she hates going to church because she doesn't understand what's going on, and John doesn't have any interest because he says there aren't any young people his age who attend."

Appearing sorrowful, Basil stated, "Sometimes I feel like it's my fault. I'm certain that my attitude toward religion hasn't helped... and at other times, I feel as if we both share some of the blame because maybe we haven't given the Greek Orthodox Church a fair chance. Whatever the reason, all I know is that, as a family, we're now at a point where I'm almost willing to do anything to correct this situation including finding a church home. Incidentally, we just found out that we will be moving again in a few months to a bigger city and I've made some preliminary inquiries about this area. I'm told that this city has several Greek Orthodox Churches. Rather than change religions at this point in our kid's lives, we've sort of decided to give it one more try. But if we can't find a Greek Orthodox Church that feels right this time, I'm sure we'll be making a change."

Challenges Related to Adolescence

While most intermarried couples are not as conflicted over their cultural and religious differences at this stage of the family life cycle, Basil and Jane's difficulties afford us a glimpse at many of the challenges that intermarried couples and their families can encounter. The following information serves to complement this conversation while offering a clearer understanding of the primary challenges that intermarried parents have reported facing when their children reach adolescence.

- Early family of origin experiences tend to play an important role in both an adolescent's impressions about culture and religion, and his/her continuing efforts to develop a cultural and religious identity. Basil and Jane's conversation reinforce this point. In their case, it is not surprising that their children were unable to relate to the Greek Orthodox Church. Their father's prolonged indifference toward religion, together with both parents' persistent feuding, in all probability served to negatively impact their children's perception of religion and culture.

- Adolescence is a time when everything is questioned, including culture and religion. As such, intermarried parents should expect their teenagers to both scrutinize and question their parents' cultural and religious values and beliefs. Parents who lack knowledge about their respective religious traditions, who have conflicted feelings over their religious and cultural differences, will likely fail miserably at addressing their adolescent's religious questions and needs.

- If adolescents are raised in an intercultural, intermarried family that is conflicted over culture and religion, and this conflict persists unchecked, then it is significantly more probable that they will reject the value of culture and religion altogether, or be influenced by their peers' perceptions of culture and religion.

- Parents must remember that actions speak louder than words. If teenagers discern that their parents are saying one thing to them regarding the value of religion and culture, and demonstrating another, their efforts to develop a strong religious and cultural identity will be negatively impacted. When parents fail to celebrate their cultural differences or live out their religious beliefs, their children's religious and cultural development will be generally impacted.

- Intermarried parents who have a sound understanding of each others' religious tradition, and are generally in agreement about religious matters, are in a better position to address the adolescent's religious questions. Parents, who have been in agreement about their religious and cultural differences and have offered clear messages to their children regarding religion and culture, will likely encounter fewer and less intense challenges.

- Permitting adolescents the latitude to question religious beliefs can prove to be a necessary part of their efforts to personalize their religious beliefs. Inter-Christian parents should welcome questions from their adolescents, and view their questions as opportunities for all members of the family to develop a deeper cultural and religious identity.

- Parents must try to help their adolescents develop a respect for other faith groups while also helping them to grow into a personal faith commitment in the church where they were baptized. When parents remind adolescents that they are part of a rich religious tradition that can facilitate a meaningful relationship with God, this positive emphasis assists them in discerning the value and worth of being religious. If parents spend most of their time disparaging other religions and cultural groups, such activity may simply serve to reduce adolescents' respect for their religious and cultural heritage.

- Research also suggests that if only one parent has a strong cultural and/or religious identity, then it is probable that adolescents will embrace the dominant parent's cultural and religious preferences. Adolescents who tended to identify with only one parent's cultural background may at a later stage in life discover and search out information about the other parent's cultural and religious background.

When Children Begin Leaving Home

Anastasia, age 52, is Greek Orthodox, and is married to Norm, age 54, a non-practicing Presbyterian. They have been together for nearly 25 years and live near to a large northeastern city. Both partners have successful careers. Anastasia is a graphics artist and Norm is an attorney. The couple has three young adult children, Gus, age 24, Tina, age 22, and Sam, age 20.

This couple admitted to having experienced some mild disagreements "over the years" related to their religious and cultural differences, "but nothing of consequence." Two of their children have accepted jobs in other parts of the country and have recently left home while their youngest son is away at college. "The house seems so empty these days," remarked Anastasia with a perceptible hint of sadness in her voice. Since the couple seemed focused on this topic, they were asked to reflect upon the challenges they had experienced over the past few years as their children have grown and left home.

Anastasia looked at her husband and noted that he was reserving comment so she begins with the following observations. "There have been many challenges, but I suppose the ones you want to know about are related to our family's religious struggles. So, I guess I'll start there. It's been hard for me. Norm is a good husband, and a great father. However, if I could change one thing about him, it might have been his attitude about religion…. He's never really shown much interest in attending church services and that's caused me to carry some sadness around in my heart…. I wish I could share this part of my life with him, but he has always made it clear that organized religion hasn't ever done much for him."

Norm appeared to be listening attentively. When Anastasia finished her thoughts, he made the following comments. "I suppose I need to offer some sort of a rejoinder at this point." We all laugh again.

"What can I say, I've never been a religious person. My parents weren't very religious, and we hardly went to church when I was a kid. And when we did go, it was only on special occasions like weddings and funerals and, maybe an occasional Christmas, but that was it. So, religion was never much of a part of my life.... Moreover, it's not that I haven't supported Anastasia's desire to attend church, because I don't mind it, and even respect it. Nevertheless, it's not my thing on Sunday mornings. I'd rather take a walk, or sit in the backyard and read the Sunday paper. So I guess there has always been this subtle undercurrent of tension on Sundays and holidays over the issue of religion in our lives."

"It's not that I haven't accepted Norm's attitudes about religion. I guess I really have," Anastasia interjected abruptly. "But the hard part is the kids. None of them go to church anymore. In fact, it's been several years since any of them really went regularly... I think our daughter might one day return to church because she's still semi-active, but I have serious doubts about our two sons' interest in the church. That makes me feel angry and sad at the same time. And what makes things worse is that Gus has begun attending a different church."

"I know how you feel, Sia," Norm stated affirming his wife's feelings. "But they're adults now, we can't make them go if they don't want to go."

"You don't understand Norm... I know we can't tell them what to do anymore.... I just think that we've somehow failed them in this part of their lives. And I also see this somehow separating us all from one another.... Oh, I don't know. These things seem so complicated these days. It wasn't so difficult when they lived under our roof. I could insist they come with me once in a while. But not now, and that hurts…. It's different now," related Anastasia.

Norm placed his arm around his wife, who was visibly upset, and stated, "You can't tell me they might not come back to the church with absolute certainty. You said yourself that Gus is attending another church, and Tina comes once in a while…. It's not that bad. Besides, they're all good kids. They've got good educations, and it looks as if they'll all contribute something positive to society."

Her husband's comments seemed to comfort Anastasia as she wiped the tears from her eyes. "I guess you're right. But it's still unsettling."

Challenges Related to Young Adulthood

- Typically speaking, children in our culture who reach young adulthood are busy individuating[2] from their family of origin, while parents are generally busy assisting and supporting them in their efforts to separate themselves.

- Young adults and parents are also actively retooling the nature of their relationships, forming more symmetrical relationships (adult to adult) and less complimentary relationships (adult to child).

- When young adults do separate, they tend to separate from their family of origin, as well as the cultural, religious, and community structures of their youth. This does not necessarily imply that young adults will discard their cultural and religious roots since in most cases this does not happen. Young adults are simply creating enough space between themselves and their parents to afford themselves ample room to make independent choices and decisions about important matters such as culture and religion. Moreover, if parents are too intrusive and seek to impose their values on their young adult children, they may cause tension or a cut-off to occur between the young adult and themselves.

- Unlike adolescents who busy themselves experimenting and testing out new ideas, most young adults are beginning to form the basis of a solid and stable life structure and cultural identity which will ultimately assist them in their efforts to make crucial decisions about their career and future mate.

- Because of their family of origin experiences and peer group influences young adults' perceptions of culture and religion can be grouped under one of the following four categories.[3]

1. Some young adults will primarily be labeled "majority group identifiers" and tend to identify with the parent who is from the dominant culture and may or may not identify with the other parent who is from a minority culture.

2. Some young adults will be labeled "minority group identifiers" and essentially identify with the minority ethnic, racial, or religious background of one of his/her parents. In these instances, the young adult may or may not acknowledge his/her other parent's background.

3. Some young adults will embrace a "universalizes/ disaffiliates: none of the above" attitude toward culture and religion, and tend to create their own values, rituals and identity irrespective of their parent's cultural and religious backgrounds. These types of young adults may refuse to accept any labels or create a distinct label that differentiates them from any childhood cultural and religious labels.

4. Some young adults are "synthesizers." These types of young adults strive to bring together and integrate both their parents' cultural and religious backgrounds. They acknowledge that both their parents have influenced their perceptions of culture and religion.

- As young adult children appear to be making decisions about religion and culture, it can be a particularly unsettling time for all members of the nuclear family. If parents have not come to terms with their religious differences, old wounds will generally surface and irritate their marriage – especially if their adult children make decisions about religion that appear to be related to parents' unresolved religious differences. In this case, couples might be prone to assign blame and reopen old arguments.

- Parents' relationships with their adult children might also be affected. In this case, parents with strong opinions about religion can potentially drive a wedge between themselves and their children. Adult children might pretend to espouse certain religious affiliations to please their parents. They might also resent covert and overt intrusions into this part of their lives that could negatively color their relationship. In some instances, cut-offs might also take place when irreconcilable differences over religion and culture exist between a parent(s) and a young adult child.

After the Last Child Has Left Home

Michael, age 65, and Roberta, age 63, have been married for 35 years. Michael is Greek Orthodox and proudly points out that he "emigrated from the Island of Rhodes when he was fifteen years old." Roberta has a Lutheran background and was born in a small city in the Midwest. The couple have three children and six grandchildren.

While Roberta never converted to Greek Orthodoxy, upon the arrival of their first child, she determined to attend the Greek Orthodox Church "for my children and family's sake." Roberta also stated, "Michael is a very proud, strong-willed man. So, to keep the peace, I decided that I should attend the Greek Orthodox Church and consent to having our children baptized in the Greek Church. But ever since the kids have left home, I've begun attending my church more."

At this juncture, Michael abruptly broke into the conversation. "I will tell you honestly, I wouldn't recommend a mixed marriage to others. It's been very hard…. I love Roberta with all my heart, and always will. But the subjects of religion and culture have constantly created friction in our marriage. Roberta says that I'm strong-willed, but she can be just as stubborn."

"You'll get no argument from me," Roberta crisply stated. "Now that the kids have left home, I have decided to attend my church more often, because I feel more at home there. For some reason, I've never been able to feel the same level of comfort in the Greek Church. I don't know, maybe it's got something to do with how I've always felt when I've gone to Michael's Church, sort of like an outsider."

"I don't understand that last comment," Michael stated with some irritation. "I've told her this many times. The people at church have always been nice to her, and welcomed her. So when she makes this point, I get confused and a little bit angry."

"How could you understand? You're Greek. So, it's not the same for you Michael. But just imagine this, how do you think you might feel if you attended my church all these years. Don't you suppose you'd feel a little out of place," asked Roberta.

Michael was visibly annoyed by this last comment and responded. "My dear, I wouldn't have attended your church."

"This is how it's always been when it comes to religion and culture," Roberta retorted. "You just expect me to give up who I am. Well, I did that for many years for our children's sake and to keep peace in our family. I can't do it any longer. I need to be in a church where I feel comfortable at this time in my life."

Michael asked, "What do you mean when you use the word, 'comfortable?' Can't you pray in the Orthodox Church? Can't you sing in the Orthodox Church? Don't you have friends in the Orthodox Church? I don't understand…. It hurts me Roberta, when you choose to go to the Lutheran Church on Sundays."

Roberta seemed moved by this last statement and responded. "I know it hurts you Michael. But it's what I need now. Why don't we alternate? We could go to the Greek Church one Sunday and the Lutheran Church the next Sunday. Can't you do that for me?"

Visibly angry, Michael stated, "I could, but I won't. I'm not interested in making that kind of a change in my life now."

"And neither am I interested in staying in the Greek Church the rest of my life. I need more," said Roberta.

Challenges After the Last Child Leaves Home
- In most instances, spouses at this stage of the marital life cycle have settled into comfortable patterns that suit both them and their mates. The challenges that their cultural and religious differences posed during earlier stages in the marital life cycle generally have been resolved.
- In some instances, spouses who have failed to resolve and negotiate their cultural and religious differences may consider worshipping in different churches and/or renewing cultural ties that have been ignored for years while raising their children.
- In a few instances, some couples' religious and cultural differences may prompt one or both spouses to consider separation and divorce once the last child has left home. With the previous focus on their children gone, these couples may question the value and wisdom of remaining in a relationship that is conflicted over religion and culture. In addition, in the case where they choose to remain together, marital and family well-being generally do not improve markedly.
- Finding ways of coping with the loneliness and separation that their lingering cultural and religious differences have created can impact individual well-being and function to negatively influence their children's and grandchildren's attitudes and perceptions of religion and/or ethnicity.
- In cases where couples appear to be caught within these types of irreconcilable differences, experience suggests that matters will not improve. However, all is not lost and change can occur if both desire change. Turning to God and allowing Him to remove their seemingly immovable difficulties is crucial at this time. Where their own efforts have proven inadequate, God's forgiveness, mercy, and love can loosen things up and allow them to view their differences from another per-

spective. As God's life-changing grace touches their lives, behavioral changes occur that serve to improve individual, couple, and family well-being.

Summary

Results from the IRP clearly suggest that most intermarried couples that attend the Orthodox Church will encounter challenges related to their religious and cultural differences. Some couples will only experience mild challenges while others will encounter challenges of a more serious nature.

Results also suggest that an early awareness of the potential challenges that intermarried couples might confront could assist them in finding prayerful resolutions. A tendency to avoid life cycle challenges was generally considered an ineffective approach. When couples ignored challenges related to their religious and cultural differences in one stage of the family life cycle, they reported that these differences often turned into difficulties that festered and grew over time. However, when couples prayerfully sought mutually satisfying resolutions, their efforts proved to have a positive effect on the present and future quality of their lives. As one respondent stated, "I wasn't prepared for all the difficulties we would have over our religious and cultural differences. I wish I was. But I'm glad that we didn't ignore them. Ignoring them would have probably been a serious mistake for us. I would remind every intermarried couple that if they are having any problems related to their religious and culture differences, they should address them. If they don't, they won't go away. They will only grow bigger and more troublesome."

Chapter Ten

BALANCING STRATEGIES [1]

> The married are to be admonished to bear with mutual patience the things in which they sometimes displease each other, and to assist each other to salvation by mutual encouragement. – *St. Gregory the Great*

Despite describing numerous personal, couple, family and extended family challenges, most participants also portrayed their marriages in essentially functional, positive terms. Moreover, when they were asked to describe the balancing strategies they utilized to assist them in their efforts to resolve their religious and cultural differences, the following strategies were mentioned.

Premarital Discussions

In many instances, participants indicated that premarital discussions were considered key to their efforts to deal with their religious and cultural differences. "We sat down and discussed religious concerns before we got married, and that made a big difference," stated one participant. "And even though it got sort of hot and upsetting, I'm glad we did it because the talk really cleared the air and made us both feel more comfortable with the religious concerns that other couples struggle with after marriage." Heart-to-heart discussions appeared to allow each individual the latitude to accept certain realities before marriage, as well as affording each person the opportunity to make an honest, informed decision about entering an inter-

Christian, intercultural marriage. Reflecting on the benefits of some premarital conversation, another participant stated, "I was kind of nervous about marrying him. I knew that my Greek Orthodox faith was important to me, and if we couldn't somehow resolve our differences regarding religion, well I think I was prepared to break off the engagement. But thank God, the talk helped, and the air was cleared so we could both feel good about proceeding forward with our plans to get married."

These discussions also seemed to assist spouses in their efforts to begin discerning and respecting the private side of their spouse's religious and cultural experience. The following quote illustrates this. "I knew that she was close to her religion, but I didn't really know how close until after we started talking more about religion. It's a real personal and private thing that I might never fully understand because I'm not as religious as she is. But it's also one of the things that really attracted me to her. I think down deep I really wanted someone who was religious with whom I could share my life and have a family."

Communication After Marriage

Throughout the marital life cycle, continued communication leads to increased understanding and more intimacy was deemed absolutely essential to marital and family stability. "When I look back at the twelve years that we've been married," stated one respondent, "I can point out when and where we had the most difficulties. It was when we weren't communicating. So in our case, one key has always been consistent communication." Another respondent shared the following insights, "When we're communicating life is good between us, and when we're not, well even the simplest things can't be resolved. And that also applies to the decisions we've struggled with regarding religion and culture."

Learning the value of communication as well as when to communicate about certain issues was also deemed important. The following observations illustrate this point. "Before marriage we talked about the similarities between our two churches and what the subtle differences were. We didn't talk about raising the kids Catholic or Orthodox until the point where we were having our daughter because we weren't sure we were going to have children. So we said, why make this non-issue an issue. People were bombarding us with all sorts of comments, but we continued to ignore them and did not talk about children until we decided to get pregnant. I guess, for us, when the time was right, we began talking about having children, and that's when the subject of baptism and church came up. That worked for us, and we continue to do much the same thing now."

A Work in Progress

After marriage, spouses also indicated that it was important for them to acknowledge that their marriages are "a work in progress." For example, while describing this dimension of her inter-Christian, intercultural marriage, one respondent stated, "After twenty years of being with him, sometimes I still don't know exactly what he means. It's like what kind of tone of voice was that. Was that sarcastic or was that serious? Or why did you roll your eyes at me like that. Were you joking, or what? And he's like confused because I don't know. But sometimes I still discover things about him that confuse and amaze me. So we always have room for learning, and that's true of our religious differences." Expecting disagreements to surface and challenge them throughout the marital life cycle was deemed an important acknowledgement. "And it doesn't really end," stated one participant. "We still have things come up regarding religion. Maybe not the kinds of hurdles that we had early on, but there are hurdles that still exist because life changes and new challenges occur because of these changes."

Patience

Patience was frequently mentioned as an invaluable virtue that helped these couples grapple with their religious and cultural differences. Specifically, these couples described how time and patience often functioned to allow a softening of attitudes and a different perspective to emerge between them with regards to their inter-Christian and intercultural differences. Along these same lines, being patient and discerning as to when to discuss their differences, and what differences needed to be addressed, were considered important. While describing the value that patience played in her relationship, one respondent offered the following reflections, "It definitely took time, and I realized very early on that we wouldn't develop a good understanding about our religious and ethnic differences overnight. But I was patient and didn't push the process too much, and I found that he started coming around regarding the religious and cultural thing. And now he comes to church with me once in a while and we share some of the Greek traditions, and I'm careful not to push him too much.... Patience really is a virtue in these marriages"

A Spirit of Exploration and Experimentation

During the first few years of marriage, some couples chose to experiment and visit different types of churches in their efforts to cope with their differences and find a church home. One respondent recalled the following struggles that she and her spouse encountered during the first few years of their marriage with regards to religion. "We were really having a lot of trouble over our religious differences, and I prayed about this and came to the conclusion that God didn't want us to be in conflict over religion. So we started going to other churches, you know kind of experimenting and exploring other options. But we couldn't settle on a religion that suited us both. Either there was too much ritual for him or not enough for me. And I think that this was healthy for us because it took some tension out of our marriage. We both began to respect each other's different religious needs. So now, we essentially worship in separate churches, but try to share our common faith in Christ."

While most participants did not describe this level of experimentation and exploration, many alluded to lesser forms of
experimentation and exploration with regard to religion and
cultural matters. Many described how they had worked in order to integrate their religious and cultural backgrounds to facilitate mutual participation that would enrich and broaden
their lives. While reflecting on one couple's eating habits, one
respondent stated, "We now love feta cheese and hamburgers."
Others talked about sharing their knowledge of Greek and Italian or Greek and Spanish. Others described how icons and incense, together with a renewed knowledge of the scriptures
had enhanced their religious and spiritual lives as individuals
and couples.

Mutual Love

The mutual love participants had for one another was viewed
as one of the chief ways that these couples overcame their differences and were able to grow from them. In one instance, a
non-Greek participant stated that she had begun to learn Greek
because she always wanted to know another language, and out
of the love she had for her spouse and his extended family. In
another instance, a Greek Orthodox participant stated, "My love
for my wife has helped me value and respect what's different
about us. Without the love that we have for each other, I don't
think we would have benefited from our differences. They
might have just become insurmountable issues that might have
driven a wedge between us."

Acceptance

Participants repeatedly observed that an acceptance of each
other's inherent differences – including each other's religious
and cultural differences is also important. They further warned
that anything short of this could potentially be construed as
selfish and disrespectful behavior that could damage their
marriages. For instance, consider the following observations

made by one respondent who tried to explain the value of acceptance. "And I wouldn't say to my husband, 'You've got to come over to my side,' because I love him, and I love what he has become, and what his faith has made him. I mean, we both believe in God, and God made both of us. So God is going to love us both, no matter if we are Catholic or Orthodox. And this is something that I had to ask myself before marriage, 'can you love him and accept him for who he is?' And if I had doubted this, I wouldn't have married him. After all, I met him when he was 28 years old. He was a grown man. And I couldn't ask him to come over to my side. Either I love him for who he is, or not at all. And more than this, I fell in love with this man, not some ideal in my head. Marriage is not about jumping into something with two feet. It's like jumping in with four feet and learning to accept each other for who we are and from this comes intimacy and love."

A Minimizing/Maximizing Process

Minimizing their religious differences and maximizing the benefits derived from being religious was another invaluable balancing strategy that many of these couples utilized to assist them with their religious and cultural differences. "Being open to discussion has helped us in dealing with our religious differences, but discussion can only take you so far. What I mean is that we do have differences and these differences could certainly become issues if we let them. But we don't because that would simply divide and conquer us as a couple. So we've learned on some issues to 'agree to disagree,' on others to simply accept our differences, and on still others, to look for what we share in common as Christians. In fact, if I were to guess, maybe this last approach has worked best for us. We really try and look for the things we share in common as Christians and not take issue with our religious differences because it's like I already said, it just divides us and makes things difficult. I'm Greek Orthodox, and always will be. He's Baptist, and always will be. I try and live an Orthodox lifestyle without judging his Baptist approach to religion."

Compromise

Compromise was repeatedly mentioned as being important to these types of couples. While discussing how one couple determined how much Greek and English to ask their priest to use during their baby's baptism, one respondent offered the following observations. "And I knew that some Greek was important to my husband and his family, but most of our guests were going to be non-Greek Orthodox people, so we talked about it, and we reached a really good compromise with Father Tom's help." A recognition that a give-and-take attitude will help couples move beyond their differences and toward some healthy consensus, regarding their religious and cultural differences was constantly mentioned as important to the stability of marriages. As such, it was not unusual to hear statements like the following, "We give and take, that's one of the things that makes our marriage and family work." Although compromise was considered important, participants also indicated that compromise of the type that did not violate their religious conscience was of crucial importance to them. While reflecting on this, one respondent stated, "My grandmother was not Greek Orthodox, and my *Papou* forced her to deny who she was and become Greek Orthodox. And I saw how she resented that. So, I wouldn't ever think to force my husband to change something that he believed in deeply just to make me happy. If we are really going to be happy, and develop more love and caring between us, then we have to respect what's important to each other, try to honor our differences, and not allow what's sacred and important to each of us to be compromised."

Humor

Using humor to deflect the tension and manage their disagreements over their religious and cultural differences was also deemed useful. In an effort to make this latter point, one participant stated, "We used to make a fuss over some of our religious differences, but as time passed we've learned to also see the lighter side of things in our marriage. Not taking everything so seriously has taken the edge off our conversations and put things into a proper perspective." Elsewhere, another respondent stated, "We used to have some real nasty verbal battles over my Wednesday and Friday fasting habits. After a particularly upsetting one, I went to see Father Demetri for some advice and he said, 'I can see you very clearly now. Poor, pious, holy Sophia defending her fasting habits while shooting verbal darts into her husband. Now that's something to think about.' Then he looked at me. At first, I didn't get it. But when I did, we both had a real belly laugh. Ever since that comment, whenever Jack and I are closing in on an argument that's related to my fasting habits, I think of Father's comments and how we laughed together that day, and I can't help but smile."

Fairness

As a result of their religious and cultural differences, intermarried couples must make more adjustments than single-church couples to make their marriages work. When spouses felt that their mates took both partners' religious and cultural preferences and needs into consideration, they were able to bridge their differences and find some common ground. As one respondent stated, "If either of us thinks that the other is not being fair, then problems erupt. This spirit of fair play has often made a difference in our lives, and that definitely applies to our struggles to work through our religious and cultural differences."

Freedom to Choose

Couples frequently alluded to certain irreconcilable differences that could not be compromised. In these instances, participants agreed to disagree for the sake of individual, couple, and family well-being. As such, spouses repeatedly stated that the freedom to choose with regards to religion and spirituality was highly valued. Spouses who placed a moderate to high value on religion, and were married to someone with a low level of religiosity, realized that they needed to accept their partners' indifference to religion and vice-versa. Spouses who had a strong ethnic identity struggled either to accept their mates' indifference toward ethnicity or their partners' attachment to another ethnic tradition. Spouses also valued each other's freedom to choose how much they would get involved in each other's religious and cultural traditions, and viewed force and manipulation as an unacceptable and unhealthy response. In short, spouses tried to give each other the latitude to be true to their own religious and cultural preferences while also respecting their partner's religious and cultural sensitivities.

Healthy Boundaries

Developing healthy boundaries between the couple and their extended families in order to prevent any unwanted extended family intrusions was also listed as important. In this case, couples described how they struggled to balance their own marital and family needs while also seeking to respect and honor their extended family's needs and feelings. "I really love my mother," stated one respondent, "but she can be a little pushy at times. Let me give you an example. After the wedding, and on the way to the reception, she came up to me and stated that she was looking forward to seeing us in church after the honeymoon. Well, this was a very awkward moment, and I didn't want to tell her then and there, but I knew I had no choice. So, I took her off to the side, gave her a hug, and then told her that Maria and I had decided to attend the Greek Church together. I also told her that on occasion we would be praying at St. Mary's. Well, I could tell from the expression on her face that this didn't sit well with her at first, but we managed to work it out without any lingering bad feelings when we returned from Barbados where we honeymooned."

Praying Together

Praying together was also considered invaluable in their efforts to bridge the distance between spouses as a result of their religious and cultural differences. In an effort to describe the value of prayer, one respondent made the following statement: "During the few times that we reached an impasse regarding questions like where we would worship and where we would baptize the children, prayer helped more than anything else. We just prayed together and asked God to help us make some healthy decisions, and He did." In another group, the following statements were made. "We believe in the power of prayer. It's what has sustained us everyday, but especially during some real difficult moments. I don't care if a couple is interfaith or of one faith. If they don't pray, then they're missing one of the best opportunities that couples have to allow God into their lives. Without prayer there is no way we could have the kind of marriage we have today."

Summary

While this chapter did not allude to dysfunctional marriage patterns, its important to note that conflicted couples who participated in the IRP indicated that they often lacked adequate balancing strategies that permitted them to diffuse conflict. In consequence, these couples would often get into arguments that negatively impacted marital and family satisfaction. One respondent's comments stated it best when he observed, "Our problems over religion are like the instant replays they show on television after a botched football play. Each time the subject of religion comes up, we argue, get mad at each other, and ultimately get nowhere. Worst of all, I believe these arguments have affected our happiness. I don't think anything is going to change until we do something different. If we could learn to compromise and be more accepting and tolerant of each other, this might help."

Love, acceptance, compromise, patience, fairness, prayers, boundaries etc. all seemed to assist spouses and couples in their efforts to find some balance when imbalance had crept into their relationship due to their religious and cultural differences. These Christian virtues lay a strong foundation for healthy marriages according to results from the IRP.

Chapter Eleven

There is no relationship between human beings so close as that of husband and wife, if they are united as they ought to be. – *St John Chrysostom*

While much of what is contained in this chapter will seem a bit legalistic, this information has been included in this text for two primary reasons. First, the Orthodox Church seeks to respect other faith traditions' rules and at the same time desires to protect its own theological integrity. Second, numerous couples who participated in the IRP repeatedly indicated that they were essentially ignorant of the Orthodox Church's rules as they pertain to intermarried couples and thus desired this information.

Over the centuries, the Orthodox Church has essentially held to the position that intra-Orthodox marriages are strongly preferred to inter-Christian and inter-religious marriages for the following three reasons. First, Scripture tends to support intra-faith marriage and rejects inter-religious marriage. Second, the Church has determined that intra-Orthodox marriages have a more favorable impact on the well-being of both spouse's religious and spiritual development as compared to inter-Christian and inter-religious marriages. Third, by supporting intra-Orthodox marriages, the Church believes that it will ensure its continued survival at both a micro (parish level) and macro level (Diocesan, Archdiocesan and Patriarchal levels).

As a result, a number of canons have been promulgated over the centuries to bolster these positions. These canons serve to either discourage inter-Christian, inter-religious marriages or condemn them. The promulgation of these canons does not, however, suggest that Orthodox Christians were completely dissuaded from engaging in inter-Christian, inter-religious marriages, since historical evidence indicates otherwise.

With the steady increase in the number of intermarriages occurring between Orthodox Christians and non-Orthodox around the world, the Church has tended to modify its position regarding interfaith marriages through the use of *economia*[1] i.e., a type of theological tolerance which is sometimes utilized for pastoral reasons. Depending on the perceived pastoral needs of a given autocephalous Orthodox Church,[2] more leniency has been shown toward inter-Christian marriages and inter-religious marriages throughout the Orthodox world. For example, "the Russian and other Orthodox Churches in Europe and the Near East do not refuse the Sacraments to an Orthodox spouse married to a non-Orthodox, [or] even to a non-Christian" (Constantelos, 1997, p. 69).[3] Finally, since the Greek Orthodox Archdiocese falls under the direct jurisdiction of the Ecumenical Patriarchate, Constantinople decidedly impacts the position of the Greek Orthodox Archdiocese toward interfaith marriages.

Pastoral Directives

The following pastoral directives function to guide and facilitate the Greek Orthodox priests' work with couples who either are contemplating an inter-Christian marriage or are presently involved in an inter-Christian marriage. These directives flow out of the Orthodox Church's understanding of marriage and its desire to assist its marriages and families in their efforts to cultivate (with God's grace) an Orthodox Christian environment in their homes.

As a result of the Orthodox concept of *economia*, inter-Christian marriages between an Orthodox Christian and another Trinitarian Christian are now permitted. Briefly, the Church has made this concession because it recognizes that we live in an increasingly pluralistic society. The Church is also concerned with each member's salvation, and therefore does not desire to place any obstacle before its faithful by denying the Sacrament of Marriage to those who choose to enter an inter-Christian marriage.

Although the Orthodox Church has determined to permit inter-Christian marriages between its faithful and other Trinitarian Christians, it has done so by seeking to protect its theological integrity. To that end, the following additional pastoral directives (regarding inter-Christian marriages between Orthodox Christians and other Trinitarian Christians) have emerged.

Since the Sacrament of Marriage is a Christian ceremony, and the Orthodox Church does not perform the Sacrament of Marriage for an Orthodox Christian and an un-baptized person, non-Orthodox Christians wishing to get married in the Orthodox Church must have been baptized in the name of the Holy Trinity. In addition, the Orthodox Church also does not perform the Sacrament of Marriage for two non-Orthodox Christians. At least one individual must be Orthodox in good standing with[4] his or her parish.

In order to remain in proper canonical and spiritual standing with the Orthodox Church, Orthodox Christians must be married by an Orthodox priest, in an Orthodox Church, and in the manner prescribed by the priest's service book.

Couples marrying in the Orthodox Church must also commit themselves to baptizing and raising their children in the Orthodox Church. Orthodox Christians who choose to baptize their future children in their partner's church call into question their desire to live an Orthodox lifestyle. Such a decision effects the Orthodox partner's standing with his or her church.

Since only Orthodox Christians are permitted to participate in the Orthodox Church's sacraments, sponsors exchanging the wedding rings and crowns must be Orthodox Christians in good standing with their parish. This rule is connected to the church's understanding of the sponsor. Briefly, the sponsor is more than a legal witness. The sponsor also functions as a spokesperson for the Orthodox congregation affirming the spiritual preparedness of the couple to enter into the community of marriage.

Orthodox partners should be made aware that if their marriage is not solemnized by the Orthodox Church, they are no longer in good standing and are not permitted to receive the sacraments or participate in the sacraments as a sponsor.[5]

Double performances of the wedding service, that is, in both the Orthodox Church and another Church are not encouraged. This guideline is relaxed when an Orthodox Christian has been married outside of the Orthodox Church and wishes to return to the Orthodox Church and once again become canonically and spiritually in good standing with his or her Church. In this case, after the Orthodox priest receives permission from his bishop, the Sacrament of Marriage is performed.

Co-celebrations of the Sacrament of Marriage between Orthodox and non-Orthodox clergy are not permitted. While non-Orthodox clergy are not permitted to co-celebrate the Sacrament of Marriage with the Orthodox priest they may attend and offer a benediction to the couple as well as prayerful words of exhortation.

Inter-Christian couples that wish the presence of a non-Orthodox clergyman during the Sacrament of Marriage should make their desire known to the Orthodox pastor. He will then seek the Bishop's permission. Inter-Christian couples should also be made aware of the following additional procedures.

- The Orthodox priest will extend an invitation to the non-Orthodox clergyman. At that time, the Orthodox priest will respectfully state that a co-celebration of the Sacrament of Marriage is not permitted, since the Orthodox Church does not permit non-Orthodox clergy to participate in the sacraments.

- The Orthodox priest will also clearly advise the guest clergyman on matters of appropriate vesture and seating (which is generally located in a prominent place on the *Solea*[6]). Additionally, he will also clearly indicate that the guest clergy will be properly acknowledged and permitted to give a benediction, and address the couple with some words, good wishes, and an exhortation at the conclusion of the Sacrament of Marriage.

- The couple should also be told that wedding invitations and newspaper announcements must clearly distinguish between the Orthodox celebrant and the guest clergy. Terms like "assisted" or "participated" should be avoided. Optional descriptors such as "was present" or "was present and subsequently gave a blessing" should be selected and utilized so as to clearly describe the non-Orthodox visiting cleric's role. In addition, Orthodox Priests who are invited to attend non-Orthodox wedding services may only attend as guests.

Inter-Christian couples are also respectfully informed that non-Orthodox Christians who marry in the Orthodox Church do not subsequently have sacramental privileges in the Orthodox Church. Because of the Orthodox Church's position on sacramental participation, only those who are in good standing canonically and spiritually have sacramental privileges. Similarly, intermarried couples should also be aware that only Orthodox Christians who are in good standing canonically and spiritually are (a) permitted an Orthodox Funeral Service, (b) and allowed to serve on the Parish Council, (c) permitted to vote in parish elections, and (d) permitted to serve as godparents or sponsors at baptisms and weddings.

Chapter Twelve

THE VALUE OF PREMARITIAL PREPARATION

When you prepare for a wedding,... before anything else,
invite Christ. – *St. John Chrysostom*

Inter-Christian couples reviewing these materials will observe that they are organized in the form of questions and answers which have emerged from the IRP. They are designed to facilitate individual and couple preparation before marriage. These materials are not intended to discourage couples from intermarrying. Such a decision is ultimately the couple's decision in prayerful consultation with trusted significant others.

Couples are encouraged to prayerfully review these materials privately and then together. By taking this approach, they will find it easier to enter into conversation around important issues that are ordinarily missed or ignored by many engaged couples that come from different religious and cultural backgrounds.

Most couples will find the conversations that result from interacting with these materials to be a profitable, enriching experience that will enhance their marital preparation process. Some may also discover that certain irreconcilable differences exist between them with respect to their religious and cultural preferences. If disagreement occurs, couples are encouraged to consult their pastors and, perhaps seek professional help. Generally, some conversation with their pastors or a qualified professional can help couples resolve their differences in a few sessions.

Ignoring these differences will generally not resolve them, but only postpone the inevitable. According to the results of the IRP, the likelihood is that these differences will eventually reappear and irritate couples after marriage. This will require couples to discuss and negotiate mutually satisfying resolutions or face continued relationship conflict.

Couples will find it more difficult after marriage to address these differences because they will generally have less time. During the first few years of marriage, newlyweds are preoccupied with building careers, buying a home, thinking about having children, and building a life together. All of which means that the best time to complete the work contained in this chapter is before marriage. When engaged inter-Christian, intercultural persons take the time to consider how their religious and cultural differences could impact their lives after marriage, their efforts can have a positive impact on couple communication, relationship quality, individual adjustment after marriage, and the well-being of a couple's future children and vice-versa.

Question 1. Have we prayerfully discussed the pros and cons of entering into an inter-Christian marriage versus a single-church marriage?

Results from the IRP suggest that many intermarried couples that wed in our churches do not carefully consider the pros and cons of becoming an inter-Christian couple versus a single-church couple. Results also suggest that a sizable number of participants believed they might have profited from some type of premarital conversation around this question so long as the discussion took place in "a no-pressure environment that respected each individual's religious needs and sensitivities."

If you have not spent quality time discussing the pros and cons of entering an inter-Christian marriage verses a single-church marriage, then you are reminded that meaningful, prayerful conversation can help in the immediate adjustment that occurs after marriage. Quoting one respondent, "During our first premarital marriage meeting with Father Nick, he came out and politely asked us why we hadn't considered becoming a single-church couple. When we informed him that we didn't think it was a very important question to us, he suggested that we consider it privately. Needless to say, I was a bit miffed and insulted by these questions, but didn't say anything. After this meeting, I mentioned how upset I was to George, and this finally prompted a heart-to-heart discussion about religion and the value of being a single-church couple. Even though we decided to remain an inter-Christian couple, I think Father Nick gave us permission to finally talk about a topic that we both desperately wanted to discuss, but didn't know how to bring up without sounding offensive. So, yes, I would strongly urge inter-Christian dating couples to do some similar soul searching before entering into an inter-Christian marriage."

If you have not considered Question 1 carefully, then you should ask yourselves why not. If you are both reasonably comfortable with the answers that emerge, then it is very likely that this question did not require your attention. If, on the other hand, you have failed to broach this question out of some hidden concern that it may create some discomfort, then it is likely that some discussion is necessary and will likely positively impact the well-being of your future marriage.

Couples who find that they are unable to agree about Question 1 might want to consult their pastors or a professional marriage counselor who has experience working with inter-Christian couples in an effort to arrive at a mutually satisfying understanding. Failure to reach a mutual understanding about this question could have a negative impact on marital satisfaction and family well-being in the future. A respondent offered, "I didn't realize how much I wanted to talk about our religious differences until after our marriage.... I wish someone had urged us to consider our religious differences before marriage. I'm sure discussion would have helped us avoid some of the arguments and disappointments that we had after marriage, related to our religious differences."

*Question 2. Have we prayerfully discussed the pros and cons of
becoming an inter-Christian family versus a single-church family?*

Results from the IRP also suggest that many couples who
get married in our churches have failed to carefully, honestly,
and prayerfully consider the pros and cons of becoming an inter-Christian family versus an single-church family. "It was one
thing to enter a mixed marriage," stated one respondent, "and
a whole new kind of experience when we started thinking about
having a family. Suddenly all these new issues began coming
up like names, our children's baptism and grandparent pressures." Couples considering intermarrying religiously should
consider this question since results from the IRP suggest they
will most likely encounter this issue under complex, difficult
circumstances after marriage.

Additionally, if after considering this issue carefully, a couple
chooses to raise their future children in an inter-Christian environment, these initial conversations will have provided them
with a less stressful beginning point. Opening this dialogue
early in the relationship will be helpful if and when circumstances change. "I can't even imagine the kind of arguing we
would have had if we hadn't talked about the baptism of our
future children before our marriage. I'll tell you, it would have
been miserable. So I thank God that we talked about things
before hand, because he's real religious and so am I." Do not
underestimate the importance of some conversation around this
issue, since unspoken assumptions can create future marital
and family unrest. The following brief exchange between two
IRP respondents who were married for twenty years illustrates
this point.

Sophia: "We should have considered becoming a one church
family more carefully before getting married because we ended
up creating some problems for us and our children."

Frank: "I'll be even more concise, if I had it to do over again, I
would not have considered an inter-Christian marriage and family."

Sophia: "All our children are sort of indifferent toward religion these days, and I can't help thinking that it's got something to do with the way we projected religion in our household."

Frank: "I couldn't agree with you more. We are a good example of an inter-Christian couple who should have strongly considered becoming a one church family."

Both spouses were convinced that if they had spent some quality time discussing the value of becoming an interfaith couple versus a single-church couple, many of their family conflicts over religious issues might have been averted. They also believed that they would have likely opted to become a single-church family by the time the first child was old enough to enter Sunday School.

Question 3. Have I been entirely honest with myself about entering an inter-Christian marriage?

Along with the focus groups that IRP couples participated in, couples were asked to complete a written survey. One question in this survey asked them to choose the primary factor – from a list of choices –, which motivated them to get married. Results indicate that 98% reported they married their spouse because they loved him or her. Other research projects confirm this finding. Couples in our culture generally get married because they love one another. But love can sometimes be blind, and engaged persons should remember the old saying, "what love conceals, time reveals," since love can blind engaged persons to certain realities. Furthermore, results from the IRP confirm this point.

Before marriage, some IRP respondents indicate that they loved their partner so deeply that they were willing to ignore certain uncomfortable feelings and concerns connected to their religious differences. One such individual stated, "We were so blinded by our love that we never honestly wanted to consider our religious differences carefully before marriage. All we wanted to do is get married, then sort all the religious stuff out

later. That was a big mistake. I'd advise couples to do this before marriage." Elsewhere, another participant stated, "Love can
be really blind. Before marriage, all I could see was how much I
loved him, and the rest, like my religious needs, seemed so ir-
relevant at the time. From hindsight, I can say that was a big
oversight. I should have considered my needs more carefully,
and been more honest with him and myself. It would have saved
us both a lot of grief during our first few years of marriage."

After the honeymoon is over, and somewhere into the first
year of marriage, some intermarried spouses experience a com-
bination of guilt and regrets because they failed to be honest
with themselves and their spouse before marriage regarding
their religious needs and expectations. "I really felt badly for
the longest time after we got married because I wasn't honest
with Keith and myself about the important place that religion
has in my life. So, when we got married and he wanted us to go
to his church, I was kicking myself all the way to the church
doors each Sunday for not saying something about my religion and how important it is to me. But we worked things out.
I just had to say something eventually. And I did. But it could
have led to a very ugly mess if he didn't understand. I'd suggest that couples try to do this before marriage." Another IRP
participant stated, "I never mentioned my concerns because
we were in love, and I thought that love would help me accept
some of the concessions my spouse was asking me to accept,
but it didn't. Things got especially difficult when we started
talking about children." As these statements suggest, even before marriage, dating partners may feel a sense of personal discomfort about (a) praying in separate churches, (b) praying in
their spouses' church and, (c) raising their children in an inter-
Christian environment, but fail to be honest with themselves.
Moreover, many spouses regret ignoring these concerns before
marriage, and believe that they should have worked through
these and other similar concerns before marriage.

Results from the IRP also suggest that when individuals did not ignore their personal needs, and the discomfort associated with disclosing their needs to their dating partner, this positively impacted their own adjustment after marriage as well as enhancing marital and family quality. This appeared to be the case because individuals who were honest with themselves had fewer issues related to their religious differences to negotiate after marriage while individuals who were not entirely honest with themselves struggled to find ways to address this omission after marriage. And while many of these types of omissions were successfully resolved after marriage, most participants repeatedly stated that some prayerful honesty with themselves before marriage might have served to make their adjustments after marriage less painful. "I knew how important my Church is to me, and if I wasn't truthful about this to myself, I would have had a hard time getting married to him," stated another IRP participant. "It wouldn't have been honest, and that would have put us off on the wrong foot. But thank God, I was able to be honest with myself about what my membership in the Presbyterian Church meant to me. Otherwise, I'm sure I would have felt badly after the marriage for keeping this a secret."

Question 4. Have I been entirely honest with my spouse about entering an inter-Christian marriage?

Just as it is important for engaged persons to be honest with themselves before entering an inter-Christian marriage, it is equally important that they are honest with their future partner. One respondent's reflections exemplify this point. "Even today, I know that if he couldn't accept this part of me, my Greek Orthodoxy, it just wouldn't work. So, I accept his religion, and he accepts mine. That's the only way it would have worked for us.... I just can't imagine not working through this issue, getting married, and then finding out that he wasn't going to respect my need to remain Greek Orthodox. It would have been very hard to deal with this – very, very hard." Another respondent stated, "Marriage is hard enough at the beginning for two people. Clearing away, any of the potential pitfalls that exist is sound logic from my perspective. This requires that engaged partners talk about the things that are bothering them which includes issues related to religion and culture. Talking to Sophia about some of my concerns about belonging to two different religions and cultures was anything but harmful. These conversations cleared the air and made our transition into married life easier."

According to the results from the IRP, the following are some reasons why it is beneficial for couples to broach their personal reservations regarding intermarriage with their partner before marriage.

- Respondents indicated that a failure to do so could result in compromising marital trust and intimacy as well as a future marriage and family religious well-being.

- IRP participants stated that honest, respectful premarital conversations afforded them the opportunity to begin developing effective balancing strategies that could assist them in resolving future disagreements related to their religious and cultural differences after marriage.

- Participants also maintained that during the premarital stage of the marital life cycle, honest dialogue is generally all that is necessary to arrest most premarital concerns, and increases the likelihood that couples will grapple with issues related with religion collaboratively and respectfully rather than in an adversarial, controlling, manipulative manner.

Question 5. How do I meet my personal religious and spiritual needs in an inter-Christian marriage?

Results from the IRP suggest that most inter-Christian spouses were repeatedly challenged to find ways of meeting their religious and spiritual needs. For example, Greek Orthodox respondents stated that they struggled to find ways of (a) introducing icons in the home, (b) fasting, (c) explaining why they felt more comfortable worshipping God in the Orthodox Church, (d) passing Orthodox traditions onto their children, and (e) adequately explaining why it was important to them that they participate in many of the Orthodox Church's rites and rituals. Many non-Orthodox respondents, especially those from a Protestant background, also stated that they struggled to find ways to explain (a) why "the sermon" was important to them, (b) why they needed to hear certain familiar hymns from their tradition, (c) why they felt uncomfortable with many of the unfamiliar rites, rules, and rituals in the Orthodox church, and (d) why the use of inordinate amounts of Greek and certain ethnic differences impeded their efforts to pray and feel a part of the worshipping community when they attended their Greek Orthodox spouse's church.

Many respondents also indicated that when they failed to find ways of meeting their personal religious needs, their religious participation waned, or stopped altogether. In these instances, discussions with their mates about religion were generally characterized as contentious and, by extension, destabilizing for each individual, the couple, and their family well-being. "You know," stated one respondent remorsefully, "all our arguments over our religious differences have really jaded my attitude toward the church and religion. Life is hard enough without having to fight on Sundays about religion. These days we find it easier to keep religion at arm's length. Maybe things may change in the future, but for now, we've been taking a vacation from religion and church attendance."

While there are no simple recipes that intermarried couples can utilize to ensure that their personal religious needs are met after marriage, results from the IRP indicated that the following strategies could prove useful to inter-Christian partners.

1. Each partner should clearly and respectfully articulate their religious needs to their partner before marriage. This generally requires that each partner be prayerfully honest with oneself, and then respectfully share any concerns he or she may have with their future spouse.

2. Partners should ask God for continued guidance. They should also understand that additional prayerful discussions will likely be needed after marriage. This is especially true when one or both partner's sense that their religious needs are either only partially being met or are entirely ignored.

3. Partners should concurrently consider their partner's and future children's religious needs. Otherwise, an inordinate amount of importance will be placed on their personal needs rather than the needs of their future family.

4. Individual partners should work toward increasing their knowledge of their own faith tradition both before and after marriage so that they can help their partner understand and respect their inherent religious needs.

5. Each partner should strive to acquire a clearer understanding of his or her partner's faith tradition. Understanding the similarities and differences of both religious traditions can help them acquire a deeper respect for each other's religious needs.

6. Both partners should understand that disrespectful, manipulative, intolerant, and controlling behaviors that seek to dismiss or deprive one's partner from meeting his or her religious needs will negatively impact marital and family success and stability. Such tactics also serve to impede one's own efforts to meet his or her religious needs.

Question 6. Is it necessary to be acquainted with my spouse's religious tradition?

Respondents involved in the IRP generally stressed the value of becoming reasonably well acquainted with both their own and their partner's religious needs and practices. "Do I know about my wife's Catholic faith? Absolutely. I think it's the only way to go as an inter-Christian couple," stated one respondent emphatically. In addition, others offered the following observations.

1. It is most helpful when spouses understand why their partner wants to display icons, burn incense, light candles, have a family Bible, read and study scripture, pray extemporaneously and without pre-authored prayers. In this manner, inter-Chris-

tian spouses develop a respectful attitude toward their own partner's needs as well as their own personal needs.

2. Familiarity with each faith tradition's rules, rituals, and rites, and how and why their own faith tradition differs, can help curb misunderstandings and hurt feelings linked to inter-Christian couples' religious differences.

3. Respondents also stated that when they took the needed time to become familiar with their spouse's faith tradition, they developed a keener understanding of their own religious needs and faith tradition and, by extension, a deeper faith in God.

Question 7. Will we worship together or apart?

This question is far more complex than it seems at face value. This is especially true when engaged persons have equally strong commitments to their faith traditions. If couples have not spent quality time discussing this question before marriage, then concerns related to this question will invariably challenge them after marriage. "We got married," stated one respondent, "and we never bothered to really discuss where we were going to go to church. Since we got married in the Greek Church, I assumed we were going to go to my church. So, three weeks after our marriage when Joe stated that we were going to the Baptist Church, we got into our first real argument. Imagine that. Our first argument was over religion. Isn't that ironic. Well today, I see where the problem was. We never bothered to discuss this issue. I assumed we were going to worship in my church and he assumed the opposite. That was a real mistake." Spending time addressing this question can prevent unnecessary disappointments after marriage.

Question 8. How do inter-Christian couples that have equally strong religious commitments decide whether they will worship apart or together?

Couples with equally strong religious commitments appear to have an especially difficult time finding ways of answering this question. Here are some typical decisions that couples have made in their efforts to address this.

In some cases, couples eventually succeed in striking a balance between individual and couple/family needs. These couples generally end up making adjustments that serve to meet both individual and couple/family needs, but not before making some compromises. For example, in the case of a Catholic/Orthodox couple, the Catholic spouse may attend a Saturday evening Mass to meet his or her personal religious needs, and then accompany their spouse and family to Divine Liturgy on Sunday morning. "It's hard to do, but I decided that I should go to early Mass on Sunday, and then join my family at the Greek Church. This seems to meet my needs, and also meets my family's needs."

Other couples may eventually become a single-church couple/family. For example, the death of grandparents or the changing religious needs of their children are two primary reasons that motivate many to become a single-church couple. "Up until recently, I was a fairly devout and active Catholic. But after my parents died, and as my kids began to grow, it became harder and harder for me to be a good Catholic and a good father. One day when our oldest began to question the value of church attendance, I realized that he needed me on Sundays. So, I finally made the decision to convert. In my heart, I felt that it was better for me to be Orthodox, than for my children's religious development to suffer."

In other instances, some couples will remain in an inter-Christian marriage but determine to worship together for the sake of their children's religious development. "I attend for the sake of my children, but I still consider myself Baptist," stated one respondent. "Maybe that will change in the future. But for now, that's the way things have to be." When the children are finally launched from the home, however, some of these couples may end up worshiping in separate churches. This is especially true when one partner has made the concession to worship in the partner's church, but has been unsuccessful in meeting his or her religious needs in the partner's faith community. "After the kids were gone, I found that I couldn't continue to attend my husband's church. I needed to return to the Orthodox Church. I know this decision has created some strain for us on Sundays but I think he's begun to understand why I had to make the change."

If inter-Christian spouses with equally strong religious commitments determine to worship together, they should be aware of the following caveats.

1. When couples decide to worship together, the spouse who has made concessions will likely feel somewhat short-changed. Conversely, the other partner will feel somewhat guilty because he or she is aware of these concessions. Both spouses are also likely to feel somewhat empty and saddened because they may discern that their religious differences prevent them from cultivating intimacy and oneness in this important dimension of their lives.

2. Many of these couples utilize their common Christian faith to help them circumvent their religious differences and disappointments. God's grace helps them make the needed adjustments to protect marital and family stability while also meeting their individual religious needs.

In other instances, because of both spouses' equally strong commitments to their faith tradition, some couples never succeed in worshiping together and generally worship in separate churches. There are numerous reasons why this occurred. Here are some common reasons that IRP participants gave. (1) Spouses do not feel comfortable worshiping in their partner's church. (2) Spouses desire to receive the sacraments regularly. (3) Spouses do not have the time to attend two church services regularly. In these cases, it is highly unlikely that these couples will ever become single-church couples/families.

Question 9. When one spouse has a strong religious commitment and the other has a weak religious commitment what are some typical challenges these couples may encounter?

When inter-Christian couples with unequal religious commitments wed, most of these couples often have an easier time deciding where they will worship. If both spouses choose to worship together, then the spouse with the weaker religious commitment will generally follow the spouse with the stronger religious commitment to his or her church. While describing how one couple chose where to worship, one IRP respondent stated, "Oh that was easy, he's the more religious one of us both, and I respected this about him before marriage. So, when it came time to select between the Greek Orthodox Church, and his Church, the choice was easy. We went to the Protestant Church." In short, results from the IRP suggest that the spouse with the nominal faith will generally attend their spouse's church, and in many instances, this spouse may consider converting to the partner's faith tradition.

These couples are not, however, insulated from certain challenges. For example, with the exception of Christmas, Easter or an occasional baptism, wedding or funeral, the rule of thumb in many of these marriages, is that the spouse with the strong religious commitment will generally attend church services alone. This also means that an important part of the strong believer's life will never be intimately shared with the nominal believer. Commenting on this, one respondent stated, "It's sometimes hard sitting in church alone Sunday after Sunday. I feel sad because I can't share my love of God with him."

These types of spouses may also experience some lingering disagreements with regards to the value of religion that could affect marital and family stability. The spouse with the strong commitment may end up becoming somewhat defensive and confrontational as a result of his or her spouse's indifference to religion. "I started pushing him to come to church with me," stated one IRP participant. "But that was a mistake. The harder I pushed, the more we became conflicted over religion. I finally took my priest's advice and stopped pushing and that helped reduce our arguments.... It's still hard, but at least we don't fight any more."

In other instances, the spouse with the weak commitment might be the one to become defensive and confrontational while the spouse with the strong faith might become discouraged and saddened by his or her partner's negative reactions toward religion. "I'm a kind of cynic when it comes to religion, and Maria knew this about me before we got married. So early on when I began challenging what she was doing, I noticed this upset her and caused some tension between us. Fortunately, I realized this was happening, and I decided to stop the questions. I still have them, but I know Maria doesn't like engaging in this type of conversation… so, even though I don't understand her need to be religious, I've grown to respect this need, and she sort of respects my indifference toward religion."

When intermarried spouses with unequal religious commitments determine to marry, they should also be cognizant of the following caveats:

1. Failure to address their unequal religious commitments before marriage can produce marital and family conflict when the issue of couple worship is eventually broached.

2. Discussions regarding religious worship should seek to respectfully consider each spouse's feelings and thoughts.

3. Reaching a mutually agreeable understanding about this issue can positively impact individual, couple and family well-being.

Question 10. Where will we pledge?

Disagreements stemming over the way couples manage, utilize, and discuss their finances are not uncommon. When couples fail to strike a mutually satisfying understanding regarding their finances, a serious marital conflict can result. It is important that inter-Christian couples discuss the manner in which they will pledge. A failure to do so may result in creating hurt feelings and unexpected marital disagreements. The following questions should be considered during this conversation.

- Can we afford to pledge to two churches?
- How will we determine what amounts to pledge to both churches?

- If we only pledge to my church, how will that affect my partner?
- If we don't pledge to my church, how will that affect me?

Question 11. How much of a Greek Orthodox home will we have?

Greek Orthodoxy is not simply something that its adherents do on Sunday morning; it is more of a lifestyle that profoundly affects each day of a person's life. Living one's Orthodox Faith is of central importance to Greek Orthodox Christians self-understanding and religious and spiritual well-being. As a result, Greek Orthodox Christians who contemplate entering into an inter-Christian marriage owe it to themselves and their future spouses to consider this question carefully with their partners. Otherwise, misunderstandings and disappointments could develop after marriage. Careful consideration of questions such as the following few should be respectfully considered and discussed:

- Where will the icons go in my inter-Christian home?
- How will my non-Orthodox partner react to the burning of incense?
- Will my partner be respectful to other Orthodox rituals and traditions that I choose to follow at home?
- What will our diet look like around the Orthodox Church's fasting periods?
- How will we pray together as a couple at home?

Question 12. In which faith tradition will the children be baptized?

The following story illustrates some of the problems that inter-Christian couples encounter when they fail to discuss the issue of baptism before the children arrive. And while this example is somewhat exaggerated, the challenges contained in this short vignette are not entirely unusual.

Sam, age 27, and Emily, age 28, have been married for two years. Emily is Roman Catholic and Sam is Greek Orthodox. Before their marriage, Sam assumed that the couple's children would likely be baptized Greek Orthodox, since they were married in the Greek Orthodox Church, but he never shared his feeling with Emily before marriage. Emily assumed that the couple would discuss this issue. As a result of their busy schedules, this couple never broached baptism until three months after the birth of their first child when Sam suddenly suggested that they make an appointment with his priest to have the child baptized. This suggestion surprised and hurt Emily, and the couple proceeded to have a serious disagreement which caused them to postpone their child's baptism.

Sam eventually succeeded in pressuring Emily into yielding and their baby was eventually baptized several months later. The baptism fell far short of being a festive event that gave both parents and extended families cause to celebrate. Throughout the process, Emily did not understand the symbolism. She felt the priest treated her in a condescending manner. She resented her in-laws efforts to disregard her ethnic background and turn the reception into "a Greek affair," and she was especially upset at how insensitive to her feelings Sam was throughout the process. Moreover, this resentment lingered even after the baptism and caused additional disagreements to surface regarding their child's religious and spiritual development.

While most baptisms are not this unsettling, scenarios like this one are not all that uncommon among inter-Christian couples. When partners from different religious and/or ethnic traditions are considering marriage, the results from the IRP suggest that they will be well served if they spend time before marriage discussing this issue carefully. The following related questions might facilitate this process.

- How will I feel if my children are baptized in my spouse's church?

- If we choose to baptize our children in my faith tradition, how will my spouse feel, and how will this decision impact our marriage?

- How will my parents react if our children are baptized in my spouse's church?

- If we choose to baptize our children in my faith tradition, how will my in-laws feel, and how will this decision affect our relationship?

Question 13. How do we help our children acquire a strong religious identity?

Results from the IRP clearly indicate that inter-Christian spouses and parents frequently espouse multicultural values, or a respect and tolerance for difference. Consequently, most intermarried parents seek to consciously infuse their children with respect and tolerance for other religious and cultural traditions especially both parents' religious and cultural traditions.

However, while results from the IRP suggest that inter-Christian couples may espouse a respect for difference, results also suggest that most couples deliberately indoctrinate their children into one faith tradition. Results also suggest that without exception, parents who made this choice reported that this decision turned out to be in the best interest of their children's religious development. Parents who remained conflicted over this issue and chose to raise their children in both spouses' churches, from hindsight, regretted their decision for the following reasons.

1. While it was not necessarily detrimental to raise their children to have respect for other religious traditions, children's religious development seems to fare better when they are raised in one faith tradition.

2. Just as children require both parents to be in agreement when it comes to other dimensions of their development, it is equally important to their children's religious well-being for the parents to be in agreement about their children's religious development.

3. Parents' mutual decision to raise their children in one church provided the children with the needed consistency and structure that they required to (a) bond to a faith tradition, and (b) develop a religious identity.

Respondents also discouraged parents from choosing to raise some of their children in one parent's faith tradition and others in the other parent's faith tradition. In these instances, respondents stated that this approach served to compromise their children and family's religious well-being. They further stated that even though such an approach may have made each partner feel better, it served to send mixed messages to their children that ultimately diluted (a) the parents' efforts to provide needed religious consistency and structure, and (b) impaired their children's efforts to bond with a faith tradition and develop a religious identity.

On the strength of this information, engaged persons contemplating an inter-Christian marriage should carefully discuss this question before marriage and come to some mutually agreeable decisions. Intermarried couples failing to do so are significantly more likely to affect their children's religious and spiritual growth in a negative manner.

Question 14. How do we deal with the questions our children will have about our inter-Christian marriage?

As children mature, they begin to ask their parents questions in an effort to piece their physical and social worlds together. Furthermore, some of these questions will inevitably be related to religious matters. Along with the questions of a religious nature that single-church parents must contend with, inter-Christian parents must also contend with an additional set of questions related to their religious differences. In short, sooner or later, six-year-old Tommy or five-year-old Loren will detect that Daddy does not receive communion with the rest of the family, or Mommy does not make the sign of the Cross, or that Daddy goes to a different church on Sunday mornings. And when this occurs, questions invariably will follow.

Before this time arrives, and it will arrive sooner than most engaged couples think, couples contemplating an inter-Christian marriage are advised to begin anticipating how they might address these questions. The following information from the IRP will hopefully assist couples in their efforts to prepare themselves for these inevitable questions.

Many parents stated that these kinds of questions were particularly difficult for them to answer. One factor making these questions difficult appears to stem from a parents' desire to protect and nurture their children's developing religious identity. "I started worrying about what I would say to my daughter when she finally got around to asking me some questions about our different religious backgrounds. What worried me is that I might say the wrong thing and give her a false impression about the way I think about my faith." To be more specific, these parents did not want to say anything that might compromise their children's efforts to bond with the faith tradition in which they were being raised. For example, one respondent stated, "When my son asked me why his father didn't receive communion, I didn't know how to handle the question. I was afraid that I might say something wrong that would affect the way he thought about his father or the way he thought about his church."

Another factor was connected to the parents' desire that their children develop a respect for both parents' religious tradition, as well as a respect and tolerance for other religious traditions. "It's been hard," stated another respondent, "walking the thin line between helping my children respect their father's religious background, and helping them develop a strong bond with their Orthodox Faith. Sometimes I'm not sure how successful we've been, and I often wonder if we're confusing them. We want them to respect and know their father's religious background, but we also want them to understand that they are Greek Orthodox."

One last complicating factor was linked to their determination that they would not allow their religious differences to divide the members of their family and compromise marital and family stability. "We are a two religion family, but we don't want this to somehow divide us. So, we've spent a lot of time helping them identify with the faith in which they've been baptized, while also reminding our children that we are all Christians. I believe that this balanced approach has helped."

Question 15. Will our ethnic and cultural differences present us with any challenges?

Ethnic and cultural backgrounds impact the way we think, feel and behave. Moreover, this occurs in subtle ways that are generally outside of our awareness. Ethnicity and culture play a role in what we prefer to eat, how we work, how we relate to others, how we feel about life, death, gender, sex, politics, money, raising children, where we choose to live, and illness. In short, the culture and ethnicity with which we identify decidedly impacts our view of the world.

Information from the IRP repeatedly reinforced these observations. Results also indicate that some premarital discussion focusing around partners' ethnic and cultural differences seemed valuable (a) to persons from different ethnic backgrounds, and (b) to couples with different degrees of ethnic attachment. Couples who put aside time to discuss their cultural and ethnic differences felt more comfortable about these differences and more self-assured that their differences would be respected after marriage. These couples also indicated that continued conversation after marriage was equally important to them in their efforts to profit from their ethnic and cultural differences. In the words of one respondent, "Taking some time to discuss how Athena's Greek heritage, and my Colombian background might create some problems for us after marriage was a great help to us. We were both concerned about how we could be respectful to both our backgrounds. Discussing our fears and concerns helped, and further discussions continue to help. I would recommend that all engaged couples talk about their cultural and ethnic differences before and after marriage." To facilitate this effort, consider using the following list of questions during your discussions:

- What about the issue of food and drink in your future home?
- What about politics? Can I live with someone who is inclined to be supportive of Turkey more than Greece?
- How much of a Greek home do I want?
- Will we speak Greek in our home?
- Will we speak any other languages?
- How much of a Greek home is acceptable to my spouse?
- How much of a non-Greek home does my spouse want?
- How much of a non-Greek home is acceptable to me?
- How will we raise our children to be respectful of both of our ethnic backgrounds and cultural differences?
- Will our future children speak Greek?
- Is it necessary to be acquainted with my future spouse's ethnic/cultural tradition?
- How will we deal with extended family members who might covertly seek to pressure us into adopting ethnic traditions?

Just how much time each couple spends on these and other similar questions will depend on how important each partner's ethnic tradition is to him or her. If one or both spouses' ethnic backgrounds are moderately to highly valued, then some respectful discussion focused on their ethnic and cultural needs will likely prove profitable. These conversations will serve to reduce future disagreements related to spouses' ethnic and cultural differences.

Finally, to determine where you currently stand with regard to the information in this chapter, consider taking the following questionnaire. This assessment tool should help you identify your weaknesses and strengths: to God's glory and your salvation. Amen.

Assessing Your Readiness to Intermarry

Each partner should read each statement and circle **Y** for "yes" and **N** for "no."

1. Have we prayerfully discussed the pros and cons of inter-marriage?　　　　　　　　　　　**Y**　　　**N**

---

1. Have we prayerfully discussed the pros and cons of becoming a single faith family?　　　　**Y**　　　**N**

---

2. Have I been entirely honest with myself about entering an inter-Christian marriage?　　　　**Y**　　　**N**

---

3. Have I been entirely honest with my spouse about entering an inter-Christian marriage?　　　**Y**　　　**N**

---

4. Have we discussed how each of us will meet our personal religious and spiritual needs in an inter-Christian marriage?　　　　　　　　　　　　　　　**Y**　　　**N**

---

5. Is it necessary to be acquainted with my spouses' religious tradition?　　　　　　　　　**Y**　　　**N**

---

6. Have we decided whether we will worship together or apart?

                                     Y   **N**

_____

7. Have we discussed our religious financial commitments?

                                     Y   **N**

_____

8. Can we afford to pledge to two churches? **Y**   **N**

_____

9. How will we determine what amounts to pledge to both churches?   **Y**   **N**

_____

10. If we only pledge to my church, will that effect my partner?

                                   Y   **N**

_____

11. If we don't pledge to my church, will that effect me?

                                   Y   **N**

_____

12. Is it important for us to consider how much of a Greek Orthodox home we will have?   **Y**   **N**

_____

13. Have we talked about where the icons will go in our home?
Y   N

_____

14. Do I know how my non-Orthodox partner will react when I burn incense?   Y   N

_____

15. Have we talked about what our diet will look like around the Orthodox Church's fasting periods?   Y   N

_____

16. Have we talked about how we will pray together as a couple in our home?   Y   N

_____

17. Have we talked about where our future children will be baptized?   Y   N

_____

18. Will I be upset if our children are baptized in my spouse's church?   Y   N

_____

19. Will my marriage be negatively impacted if I insist that we baptize and raise our children in my faith tradition?

Y   N

_____

20. Will my parents be upset if our children are baptized in my spouse's church?   Y   N

_____

21. Will my in-laws be upset if we baptize our children in my faith tradition?   Y   N

_____

22. Have we talked about how our children will develop their religious identity?   Y   N

_____

23. Have we talked about how we will deal with our future children's questions regarding our religious differences?

Y   N

_____

24. Does honoring and respecting our parents mean that we should acquiesce to their demands when it comes to making decisions about our children's religious and spiritual development?   Y   N

_____

25. Am I aware of the Orthodox Church's rules pertaining to Intermarried couples?   Y   N

_____

26. Are we aware of the Orthodox Church's rules?
                                              Y   N

_____

27. Do I know why my non-Orthodox in-laws cannot receive the sacraments in the Greek Orthodox Church?
                                              Y   N

_____

28. Should my future in-laws want information about non-Orthodox participation in the Orthodox Church's sacraments, have we discussed how we will explain the Orthodox Church's position?   Y   N

_____

29. Have we discussed how we will respect each other's cultural traditions and preferences?   Y   N

_____

30. Is it necessary to be acquainted with my future spouse's ethnic/cultural background?   Y   N

_____

Scoring: Give yourself one point for each "yes" answer. Add your scores together to arrive at a final score.

If you both score 40 or better, you are well on the way toward finding some respectful, holy agreement regarding your religious and cultural differences. But please do not assume that you will not experience some challenges related to your religious and cultural differences in the future. Instead, you might want to review your answers together to consider where your points of disagreement exist. You should also consider consulting this resource in the future should you suddenly encounter some challenges. Should you get stuck at any time, you might also consider asking your pastors for some assistance. Another option might be to log on to the Interfaith Marriage Website at www.interfaith.goarch.org.

If you both score less than 40, you should remember that your score does not indicate that your religious and cultural differences will negatively impact future marriage and family well being. However, it does suggest that you could benefit from some additional prayerful discussion regarding your religious and cultural differences. To help you, consider reviewing your answers together, along with this resource. In addition, further prayerful, respectful discussion should help. If you happen to get stuck while you are discussing your differences and cannot reach any agreement, you should consult your pastors and/or log on to the Interfaith Marriage Website for help.

The other day I was walking through an airport. There in front of me was an elderly couple. They were holding hands. I could tell they were happy and comfortable with one another. Without knowing them, it was apparent their affection was real. They touched me.

After boarding the plane and settling into my seat to fly home, I thought of these two people holding hands. "Still in love," I mumbled to myself, "despite all the trials and tribulations that this life brings." It then occurred to me, that is what all married people desire. We don't get married with the specific intention to part.

Life brings its successes and heartaches. It blesses us with one another, and from this union emerges a fuller, deeper love. Not the kind of wholesale love that we hear about in the media that reduces love to physical urges and selfish passions. This love is not simply based on making love. The love to which I am referring embodies infinitely more. In its essence, it is holy and spiritual in nature. It brings man and woman together, and through the sharing of time and the bittersweet moments that life has to offer, blesses us with oneness.

It's about the sharing of our most intimate thoughts. It's about crying over our failures, and celebrating our victories and accomplishments. It's about the willful merging of two people's dreams and aspirations into one life. It's about allowing God to shape and form two unique, distinct egos into better persons. It's about two special children of God building and shaping a holy relationship in our Lord.

It's also about raising our most precious treasure - our children. It's about holding their tiny hands and guiding their first footsteps as they walk toward adulthood. And yes, it's eventually about letting go, and observing them as they make their own way in this world.

It's about watching your son hit a baseball, your daughter learning to ride her first bicycle, blowing up their birthday balloons, tending their cut knees when they fall, and comforting them and providing direction when they fail. It's about watching them enter elementary school, middle school, high school and perhaps college, meeting the love of their life, and celebrating their marriages. It's about holding your children's children and watching the blessed process unfold once again....

As the plane lifted off the ground, I thought, this is some of the stuff that makes for a good life, and what must have been behind this elderly couples embrace. Gone are most of the reasons that caused them to embrace when they were young. In their place emerge other equally important, intimate feelings and thoughts that generate and cultivate intimacy and bonding. These are some things that we do not hear about in our youth-oriented, divorce-prone culture. But they are just as valuable and just as meaningful because they allow for healthy closure throughout the life cycle.

I began this book three years ago. God knows I put my heart and soul into it. My hope was to identify some of the challenges that intermarried couples encounter, so that these challenges might facilitate growth and togetherness. If you are conflicted at this time, please fight against the urge to be discouraged. Hang in there and keep struggling. Statistics inform us that most couples who report marital dissatisfaction today will find stability in time if they desire more, and work towards finding it. I pray that some of the ideas you have encountered in this book will empower you – in some small way – in your efforts to experience the holy mystery of two coming together and experiencing oneness: to His glory and our salvation. Amen.

Fr. Charles Joanides, Ph.D., LMFT
December 8, 2001

St. John Chrysostom, *St. John Chrysostom: On Marriage and Family Life*, Crestwood, New York: St. Vladimir's Seminary Press, 1986

Joel Crohn, *Mixed Matches: How to Create Successful Interracial, Interethnic, and Interfaith Relationships*, New York: Fawcett Columbine, 1995

William J. Doherty, *Take Back Your Marriage: Sticking Together in a World that Pulls us Apart*. New York: The Guilford Press, 2001

Paul Evdokimov, *The Sacrament of Love: The Nuptial Mystery in the Light of the Orthodox Tradition*, Crestwood, New York: St. Vladimir's Seminary Press,1995

David and Mary Ford, *Marriage as a Path to Holiness: Lives of Married Saints*, South Canaan, PA: St. Tikon's Seminary Press, 1994

Peter M. Kalellis, *After the Honeymoon: How to Maintain a Happy Marriage*, Diocese of Pittsburgh, PA: Syndesmos, 1999

Fr. John Mack, *Preserve Them O Lord,* Ben Lomond, CA: Conciliar Press, 1996

Fr. John Meyendorff, *Marriage: An Orthodox Perspective,* Crestwood, NY: St. Vladimir's Seminary Press, 1975

Charles C. Moskos, *Greeks Americans: Struggle and Success*, New Brunswick: Transaction Publishers, 1990

Howard J. Markman, Scott Stanley, & Susan L. Blumberg, *Fighting for Your Marriage: Positive Steps for Preventing Divorce and Preserving a Lasting Love*, San Francisco, CA: Jossey-Bass Publishers, 1994

Marilyn Rouvelas, *A Guide To Greek Traditions And Customs In America,* Bethesda, MD: Nea Attiki Press, 1993

Anton C. Vrame, ed, *Intermarriage: Orthodox Perspectives*, Brookline, MA: Holy Cross Orthodox Press, 1997

Judith S. Wallerstein, Julia M. Lewis, & Sandra Blakeslee, *The Unexpected Legacy of Divorce: A 25 Year Landmark Study*. New York: Hyperion, 2000

Father Kallistos Ware, *The Orthodox Way*, Crestwood, New York: St. Vladimir's Orthodox Theological Seminary, 1979

Timothy Ware, *The Orthodox Church: New Edition*, London: Penguin Books, 1997

INTRODUCTION
[1] Since the overwhelming majority of inter-married couples belonging to our churches are inter-Christian and intercultural, this guidebook has been written for these types of couples. While much of the information in this guidebook may apply to other types of intermarried couples, the specific challenges facing other types of intermarriages, such as interreligious marriages, will not be addressed in this guidebook. This resource will seek to assist inter-Christian couples that have chosen to attend a Greek Orthodox Church.
[2] You may contact Rev. Fr. Charles Joanides, Ph.D., LMFT through the Greek Orthodox Archdiocese of America in order to obtain further information about this research project.

CHAPTER ONE
[1] See Stanley S. Harakas , "Ecumenical and Pastoral Directives on Christian Marriage: The Eastern Orthodox Churches." *Intermarriage: Orthodox Perspectives*. Holy Cross Orthodox Press, Brookline, Mass, 1997, Anton C. Vrame, editor.
[2] The descriptor "interfaith marriage" is an inclusive term and refers to inter-Christian and inter-religious marriages.

CHAPTER TWO
[1] The majority of participants (92%) involved in the IRP identified themselves as having some degree of affiliation to Christianity. The comments in this section essentially refer to these respondents.

CHAPTER THREE
[1] Greek Studies scholars and Greek Orthodox theologians utilize this term to describe the interconnected relationship that exists between religion and ethnicity within the Greek Orthodox experience. Greek Orthodox Christians involved in the IRP frequently described an inter-relationship between their religious

and ethnic backgrounds. However, the degree of connection tended to vary. Participants' observations suggested that this interconnectedness tended to attenuate from one generation to the next. In these cases, (a) Christian values rather than Orthodox Christian values, and (b) dominant American values as opposed to their parents' and grandparents' old world Hellenic values assumed a more prominent role.

CHAPTER FOUR

[1] The Greek Orthodox Church receives Christians who have been baptized in the name of the Holy Trinity and in water into the Orthodox Church by Chrismation. Other Orthodox jurisdictions utilize different practices. All other converts are baptized.

CHAPTER SIX

[1] This term suggests that either one or both spouses may be primarily influenced by dominant American cultural values.

CHAPTER SEVEN

[1] The term *Yiayia* is the Greek word for grandmother.

CHAPTER EIGHT

[1] If spouses have been previously married, then the children may be part of the divorced partner's extended family. In these cases, one or more extended families can potentially influence interfaith families.

[2] The term *Papou* is the Greek word for grandfather.

CHAPTER NINE

[1] The acronym YAL stands for Young Adult League

[2] When social scientists utilize this term, they are referring to young adults' efforts to separate themselves from their parents in an effort to form their own opinions about the world around them.

[3] For more information about these four categories please refer to the following reference: Joel Crohn, *Mixed matches: How to Create Successful Interracial, Interethnic, and Interfaith Relationships*, New York: Fawcett Columbine, 1995.

CHAPTER TEN

[1] Balancing strategies are mutually agreed upon approaches that served to enhance individual, couple and family stability.

CHAPTER ELEVEN

[1] This theological concept refers to a timely deviation the Church might take from a canonically established rule. Such a decision might be made to preserve the unity of the Church and facilitate its faithfuls' religious and spiritual development.

[2] Unlike the Roman Catholic Church, which has a centralized form of government, the Orthodox Church is a family of self-governing Churches referred to as autocephalous Churches.

[3] See Demetrios J. Constantelos, "Mixed marriage in historical perspective." In *Intermarriage: Orthodox Perspectives*. Holy Cross Orthodox Press, Brookline, Mass, 1997, Anton. C. Vrame, editor.

[4] According to the Special Regulations and Uniform Parish Regulations of the GOA (Article VI, Section 1), "Any person, eighteen years of age or over, who has been baptized according to the rites of the Church, or was received into the Church through Chrismation, who lives according to the faith and canons of the Church, who has met his financial obligation to the Parish and abides by the regulations herein and the by-laws of the Parish, is a member in good standing of the Parish."

[5] The term sponsor is a generic term that can refer to either the *paranymphos* or *paranymphy* who exchanges the rings and crowns during the Sacrament of Marriage or the godparent during the Sacrament of Baptism.

[6] This is the area directly in front of the Iconostasis (Icon Screen) in all Orthodox Churches.